MW01174139

THE CAMPUS LIFE
GUIDE TO

MAKING AND KEEPING FRIENDS

Campus Life Books

THE CAMPUS LIFE
GUIDE TO
MAKING AND KEEPING FRIENDS

by CHRIS LUTES & KRIS BEARSS

A DIVISION OF CTi
CampusLife
BOOKS

ZondervanPublishingHouse
Grand Rapids, Michigan
A Division of HarperCollins*Publishers*

The Campus Life Guide to Making and Keeping Friends
Copyright © 1991 by *Campus Life Books*, a division of CTi
All rights reserved

Requests for information should be addressed to:
Zondervan Publishing House
1415 Lake Drive S.E.
Grand Rapids, Michigan 49506

Library of Congress Cataloging-in-Publication Data

Lutes, Chris.
    The Campus life guide to making and keeping friends / by Chris
Lutes and Kris Bearss.
        p. cm.
    Summary: A guide for teenagers from a Christian perspective to
making and keeping friends.
    ISBN 0-310-71021-9
    1. Teenagers—Religious life. 2. Friendship—Religious aspects—
Christianity—Juvenile literature. 3. Friendship in adolescence—
Juvenile literature. [1. Interpersonal relations. 2. Friendship.
3. Christian life.] I. Bearss, Kris. II. Title
BV4531.2.L87   1990
158'.25—dc20   90–33183
                                                                        CIP

Printed in the United States of America

91 92 93 94 / CH / 10 9 8 7 6 5 4 3 2 1

Contents

LET US INTRODUCE OURSELVES

Chris: As you can see, there are two authors listed on the cover of *The Campus Life Guide to Making and Keeping Friends*. For me, this dual authorship makes a great deal of sense. There is really no better way to test the limits and the value of friendship than through working day-to-day with someone.

Occasionally, like all friends, we'd argue as we worked on this book together: "No, no, that's not right. That doesn't belong in the book!" Then there were the all-important compromises: "Instead of dropping the entire chapter, let's just cut it in half, OK?" "OK."

Of course, there were the times of affirmation: "Hey, this is really fine. Good job!"

And, lastly, there were the relaxed, fun times we'd have during our hectic schedules at the *Campus Life* offices: "Let's take a break. Hey, Kris, can I grab you a Coke from the machine downstairs?" "No, but I'll take a grapefruit juice." Grapefruit juice? Well, I guess we all have our idiosyncracies.

All this says that Kris and I have put together a book on the hows, whys, and wherefores of friendship—and put it to the test in our own lives. The results? A guide that we hope will work for you as much as it has worked for us.

Kris: A lot of people have contributed to this book just by befriending Chris and me. We couldn't name everyone, but we did get to mention a few of the people who have shaped our lives the most. Getting to share some of my friends with you was one reason I wanted to do this book. Especially since I think friends are so important.

I was also excited because I thought Chris would be fun to work with. He was. And just talking to each other about our friendship experiences made the friendship between the two of us even better.

I wasn't really surprised at that. Past friendships tend to pave the way for making new ones and improving the ones you've got. That's what happened with us; that's what this book is all about.

PART ONE

FRIENDSHIP: WHAT'S IT ALL ABOUT?

CHAPTER 1. Friends Talk about Their Friendships

Chris: This guide is about connecting—getting together with new friends. It's also about making old relationships even better.

In order to get a handle on what "connecting" really means, I decided to talk to nine students. They gave some thoughtful ideas about how to build better friendships and overcome bad situations. They opened up a lot of friendship issues—problems and concerns that Kris and I deal with throughout this book.

Let's begin with a very basic question: Why are friendships important?

Joel: We'd die inside without them.

Cindy: Everyone needs a friend—someone they can love and someone who can love them back. It's like a security that we all need.

Can't our families perform the same function? Offer us that security?

Cindy: I don't think so. Family members can be your friends, but that's different from having a close relationship with someone your age. A friend is someone you can talk to about your problems. Sometimes you don't feel real comfortable talking to your parents or your brother or sister about such things.

Joan: It's easier to talk to a friend because she's not going to be like a parent and say, "Well, that way isn't really the best from my experience."

Isn't it hard to get to the point where you can talk over just about anything with a friend?

Todd: I don't know how it is for girls, but I think it's a lot harder for guys to open up. Even though I have a couple of best friends, I don't feel I can tell them everything. Sometimes I feel like I have to hold back even though they know everything about me.

Why is it hard to open up?

Jeff: I think we all have our fronts up. Each of us wears some kind of a mask.

Joel: I guess I'm afraid he'll think: *Joel's not as good as I thought he was.*

Todd: I think I'm scared of getting slapped in the face. I feel that people will laugh at me if I tell them certain things.

Jeff: I can relate to that. A while back, I told this friend of mine that I liked this certain girl. He said he wouldn't say a word about it to anybody. Well, before I arrived at Sunday school class one Sunday, he had told everyone that I secretly liked this girl. She was there at the time. I walked in and the whole class was giving me these funny looks. I was so embarrassed.

Did that change your relationship with your friend?

Jeff: I am a little more careful about what I say to him.

What about you girls? Have you had similar experiences?

Cindy: For the longest time, I didn't tell my best friend, Amy, that I was adopted. I felt like she wouldn't accept me if she found out. Finally I told her and, as I expected, she just didn't know how to take it. Amy started telling a lot of people that I was adopted. That hurt because I had shared this with her in secret. What she did was hard for me to deal with at first, but I got over it. And Amy was very sorry that she'd hurt me.

What about the rest of you? Is it sometimes hard to open up to your friends?

Karen: My friends and I basically have the same problems with schoolwork, guys, whatever. Knowing that makes it easier to talk about problems. I feel I can tell them just about anything.

Kim: But I agree with what Joel said earlier. I can't always tell my friends everything because they expect me to be a certain way. If I came out and told them something that contradicted the way they think about me, I feel that might change their opinion of me. They might reject me.

Karen: I really don't think a close friend would reject you for sharing something personal about yourself.

Joel: A lot of times we get too worried about what other people think. Most of the time our friends listen to us, then just forget what we said. I mean, once it's said, it's not really that big a deal. It doesn't change a friendship at all.

What about when something is a "big deal"?

Todd: I have a friend who acts hypocritical at times. Some of his actions and the way he talks really make him look bad in front of others. And yet it's hard to go up to him and say, "Look, you shouldn't act this way. You should be a little bit more mature."

Jeff: I really think we should confront our best friends about their problems. We are doing them a favor when we do, even if they are offended by what we say. I know I'd rather have someone be honest with me, tell me that I've got a problem I need to deal with, than to have that person talk about me behind my back.

Yet to be honest, I'm guilty of not confronting when I should. I have a hard time confronting people; it's difficult.

Why is it difficult to confront someone?

Joan: A lot of times I'm afraid I'll hurt someone's feelings. I have one friend who is really, really sensitive. Sometimes I say things to her, and she gets very upset and defensive.

Karen: You never know. You could have a friend who is like a wall, and everything bounces off of her. Or you might have another friend who cries every time you go to her.

Kim: I think it's important that a friend understand where you're coming from—that you're telling her this for her own good; you're not just nitpicking, not just trying to get on her nerves. If it's just a small issue, I don't think you should confront her. But if it's something that is making her life miserable or making other people's lives miserable, you should tell her about it.

Todd: When you do think it's important to confront a close friend, you always want to be tactful. You want to be kind and respect the person's feelings. Don't preach at him.

Karen: Last summer I lived in a dorm situation at a camp. My roommate and I hated each other; we just could not get along. She had a lot of personal problems. Well, the camp leaders told me that I needed to help her deal with her problems. I didn't know what to do so I just left her alone, and that made matters worse.

Then one time we did this activity where we had to try to guess what our partners were thinking. My roommate was my partner. After a while she started opening up about all of her problems. I also started telling her about my feelings, why I was struggling with my relationship with her. By the end of the session she knew what I was feeling inside, and I had a pretty good idea of what she was going through. By the end of the summer we were really good friends.

Joel: It's too bad that sometimes we have to be "forced" to confront a problem. If Karen and the other girl hadn't been given the "assignment" to sit down and talk, they might never have become friends.

Alice's friends on the swim team wondered if they should tell her that she wasn't cut out for competitive diving.

What happens when close friendships change? When, for one reason or another, that best friend is no longer around?

Karen: I had one best friend for a long, long time. For a couple of years we were always together and I didn't spend time with anybody else. Then she transferred to another school, and I felt lost. I think it's better to have more than just one close friend.

Cindy: I can relate to that. My best friend recently moved away. I met her in the fifth grade and we were always together. I guess I neglected others so I could keep close to her. Since she left, I don't have a close friend to turn to. I wish I had associated more with others. I feel lost, like Karen.

Kim: I think it's important to have a couple of close friends, but then you have to make sure you include a lot of other people, too.

Jeff: We can unknowingly push others away by getting close to just a couple of people. You know, sometimes we can be so cold to those who are new to our school or church youth group.

Kim: This past fall I was the new person, so I know what Jeff is talking about. I went into my new school and tried hard to make friends. Yet the quality just isn't there. I think by the end of the year I will have developed some close friendships. But it takes a long time. You have to be willing to go out there and try.

Do you think that some people try to push their way into a friendship too quickly?

Jeff: Yeah. I'm thinking of a guy who is sort of sickening to watch. He'll hang around certain people; he'll even imitate their actions. He will say anything or do anything just to get friends. I remember once, we were sitting around talking about rock groups. This guy came up, and one of the other guys decided to play a trick on him. He made up the name of a rock group just to see what this guy would do. Well, the guy said he had all their records and that he loved their songs. Obviously, he said this just to make an impression. The group didn't even exist. I don't think it was right to play such a mean trick on him, but it proves a point: There are some people who will do anything just to break into a group of friends.

Dave: Sometimes these people can really get on your nerves. I mean, you want to help them work through their problems. But if you show interest in them, they want to hang around you all the time. It really gets to me sometimes.

Todd: A guy who latches onto you like that is, frankly, a pain in the hind end. You want to be his friend, but pretty soon you're his best friend, you're his mother, you're his father, you're his grandfather.

Kim: I've seen people latch onto somebody who is popular. They think they're going to look good when they're with this person. But by doing this, they often never really get known for who they are. I think all of us need to work harder at being ourselves. We should make up our minds about what we really believe and value. We need to know who we are before we make friends.

Any other thoughts on handling situations where someone becomes too clingy—too possessive?

Jeff: I think it goes back to confrontation. How do you confront people who cling to you? Should you ignore the situation, hope it will go away? Or should you come out and tell this person what the problem is?

Kim: It's obvious that these people don't have a lot of self-confidence, and I feel that they really need a friend. If they're acting like that, you need to try and get a little deeper with them. Try to talk with them one-on-one. Find out what it is they're lacking in their lives. Find out what they really need from you in terms of friendship.

Let's talk about some other areas that cause problems in friendships.

Ron: Someone who won't be honest with me. For instance, I meet somebody who seems real nice and he wants to become friends. But before long I find out he's been telling me things that aren't true. That obviously destroys my trust in him.

Jeff: I hear what Ron's saying. I don't go out drinking like a lot of my friends do. On Monday mornings it's all over school that they were out partying during the weekend. Yet they'll come up and tell me they weren't. That really bothers me.

Joan: Breaking confidence is another major problem. When you tell someone something in confidence and they go and tell someone else, it's almost impossible to ever trust that person again.

Karen: I don't always want to hear a friend griping and talking about how terrible her life is. A girl like that isn't very pleasant to be around.

Todd: The friend who lives, breathes, and talks one subject really gets to me. But you can't tell the person, "I'm tired of hearing about it." After all, that one subject is what's important to him. I think sometimes you have to spend a little less time with this kind of person, so you can tolerate the time you do spend with him.

Karen: There was a girl I was friends with last year. Her whole life was cheerleading, and that's all she cared about. Well, this year she didn't make the team, and she just fell apart. No one could stand her because she'd cry whenever the subject came up. It drove us crazy. She was so obsessed, it was freaky. I tried to talk to her, tell her she needed to find something else to occupy her time, but she wouldn't listen.

Are there friendship problems you've found in yourselves?

Cindy: Snubbing my own friends was a problem I had to deal with recently. Last year I started dating this guy. I spent so much time with him that I totally ignored all my friends. I even ignored Amy, my best friend. My friends deserve to be treated better than that.

Jeff: There is a trait in me that I think is a negative. Sometimes I've run around with friends whom I got into a lot of trouble with. I'm a follower, and I just tend to do whatever anybody else does. It's important that I choose the right kind of friends because if I don't, I find myself making some big mistakes.

Let's look at the flip side of the negatives. What are some good friendship qualities?

Todd: Somebody who listens, who takes time to hear what I have to say. He doesn't necessarily have to give me advice.

The Campus Life Guide

Karen: A good friend is someone who is not so eager to talk about herself all the time.

Todd: There are times when I tell a friend something that I think is important, and he sits there with a vacant look in his eyes. I can tell he's not paying attention. It's hard to get close to people like this. They make me feel like my friendship isn't really that important to them.

Jeff: But I want a friend who will talk, too. It's a two-way street. It's a little bit of give-and-take.

Joan: Trust is important. I need to know that this friend is not going to blab everything I tell her.

Dave: Respect. He'll respect me, he'll listen to my problems, and he won't automatically feel like he has to give advice. He'll take time to listen.

Cindy: I would like a friend to accept me for who I am. For instance, if I had a lot of money, I wouldn't want her to like me for my money.

Kim: I agree with that. A lot of kids at my school will like somebody for her status. I don't think friendships based on things like money or status are really very strong. I have a friend who's in with the popular group at school. She tells me that she can't talk to these people because they'll go off and gossip about what she said.

Ron: I like a friend who's honest. Like, if you've done something wrong, your best friend will come out and tell you that there is something bothering him.

Todd: Most of all, it's good to have a Christian friend. Someone who not only talks about his faith, but who lives it.

CHAPTER 2. *But What Is Friendship?*

Friendship is: Two people sharing the same space. Gladly.

Friendship is: Stuff held in common. Enthusiastically.

Friendship is: Interests overlapping. Naturally.

Friendship is: Shared area.

If there is no simultaneous, glad sharing of the same space, there is no friendship. If there is no stuff enthusiastically held in common, the best you can hope for is acquaintance. If there is no natural overlapping of interests, there is no foundation for friendship.

Friendship happens when your life and mine intersect. When we both like baseball. When we both tune in "Leave It to Beaver" reruns. Laugh at the same stupid jokes. Understand each other's frustrations. Share each other's good times. Compare our future dreams. Talk about big ideas together. When we both like God.

Sometimes the shared area is not so great. There are friendships where the common ground is more frothy: "We both like beer." More gritty: "Where's the party?" More shallow: "Did you see that car?"

We've all seen pathetic, little one-sided friendships. All the effort comes from one direction. One guy does all the friendship work. Sometimes the common area sounds like this: "You like me a lot, and I like me a lot."

THE REWARDS OF FRIENDSHIP

"Dan and I have come to know each other so well that we can tell what is on each other's minds. When one of us has a temper flare-up, the other plays 'the thermostat' and cools him down. Dan and I are always able to carry on a conversation about something personal; we never have to worry about the other person spreading a secret around campus."

—Larry, Palos Heights, Illinois

"When I'm dealing with a problem, I can go to my friends for advice. I appreciate the way they help me step back and get an overview of the entire situation. Just doing that helps me make a better decision."

—Dan, Tampa, Florida

"Caroline has taught me to care for others and to always look for the good in people. She has also shown me how special I am, and that I have my own place and purpose in this world. Caroline has helped me discover so many things that are beautiful in life. Before I met her, I had never really appreciated a blue sky or the joy of a simple smile."

—Charlotte, Macon, Georgia

"I guess what my friend has helped me with most is my own self-esteem. He just helps me to feel better about myself."

—Todd, Marion, Illinois

Or maybe we, both of us, want to break into the same group. We both want to be considered important by Them. We're working for the same goal and we both know it. The spark of friendship ignites between us, because we share common ground: The Group. If we can just break into the inner circle.

The point being: No shared area, no friendship.

Now ask yourself: What are my friendships built on?

What are the shared areas? And maybe, just maybe, there is a hint here at improving friendship: Work at broadening the shared area in positive directions. If the only areas you have in common are cars, sports trivia, the school's most popular clique, and metal music, perhaps you can take a risky step toward conversation about life. Or about your hidden feelings—the things only you know about you.

Getting Beyond the Big "Me"

If friendship is sharing, I need to gauge my selfishness. Am I always dictating the shared areas? Am I the one to determine what our friendship holds in common? How much do my interests dominate our friendship? In short, is there any room in this friendship for you?

How much room?

We sometimes fail at friendship because the only friend foundation we can see is "Me." My likes. My dislikes. My conversation. My feelings. My small talk.

Instead: Ask. . . . Listen. . . . Look beyond the big "Me."

Think Two-sided Friendship

Sometimes friends are out of sync with each other because they have differing views of the shared area their friendship occupies. In my mind, we're close. Lots of overlap. In your mind, we're a bit more distant. I call the friendship "close." You call it "casual."

A good friend thinks of both sides of the friendship.

Sometimes the problem is extreme. I look at you and see friendship. You don't look at me at all. If your receiver is not tuned to my frequency, I may be broadcasting signals of friendship that you are not picking up. Conversely, you may be beaming a message that I don't pick up: "Get lost!" I latch on to you and call it friendship, while you try to shake me off your sleeve, calling it nuisance.

All of which is very uncomfortable for everyone concerned. Have you ever tried to tell somebody something that they just could not hear? Huh?

"Get lost! Drop dead! Vacate my space!" would not have to be said if we worked at picking up the signals ourselves. Is there a friendship foundation that we are building on? Or is this friendship just my dream?

Another thing: That other person might never even want to tell us, "Take a hike!" if we would relax more about the friendship process, and quietly, kindly, unselfishly work on the common ground, so that the "shared area" is truly shared.

Talking, Listening

What enlarges the circles of shared area? What moves strangers into acquaintance? What moves acquaintances into casual friends? What moves casual friends into better friends? Conversation.

Talking. . . . And hearing.

I think of friendship in three talk-and-hear levels:

Silly Little Facts. There are friendships where friends talk and hear on only the Silly Little Fact level.

"How's the weather?"

"Fine, thank you. And yours?"

Friendship grows as the talk-and-hear level moves from trivia to idea. Deeper conversation is not centered on how gorgeous some male rock star is, or how quickly a Ferrari can accelerate from 0 to 125, or how last night's episode unfolded.

Silly Little Facts are fine. We needn't be philosophical about "Pass the salt." But deepening friendship turns on deepening talk. And better listening.

Profound Ideas. You can tell a friendship is deepening: There's room to share ideas. You don't feel like a fool if you share a thought. You don't fear shattering the mood of triviality by saying what you think about something that matters.

Politics. . . . Your beliefs. . . . An idea that came up in

class. . . . Whatever. . . . Fill in the blank. The blank beyond the fluffy stuff.

Secret Feelings. You know you've uncovered friendship when you can say how you really feel. And the deeper the feelings, the more sensitive the area, the closer the friend. Friends who are particularly close and comfortable may at times communicate without saying a word; the feelings are mutually felt and understood.

We all need a friend or two who can talk and hear on this level.

And we'd better never betray the confidence! Being trusted with some feeling-secret is as rare a gift as finding someone you can trust with your feelings.

Friendship Is . . .

Think of friendship, then, as shared area. Two people gladly sharing the same space, simultaneously. You and I, holding stuff in common, enthusiastically. Our interests overlapping, naturally.

Friendship is:

Shared area.

And with close friends, the sharing includes feelings you can't trust to just any old stranger.

Finding the common ground to grow such friendships isn't always easy. But it's well worth the work.

—Jim Long

Friendship Levels: A Personal Story

Dad asked me how things were going between me and my friend Ruth. I told him how frustrated I was. I had thought Ruth and I were close friends, but it turned out that she didn't really want to be very close to me. I guess, I told my Dad, that any "relationship" with Ruth had just existed in my head.

My father listened as I poured out my feelings. When I finished, he sat quietly, thoughtfully, for a few moments

The Campus Life Guide

They all wished they'd been friendlier to Melvin . . . the day he brought Bruce to school.

before he said, "Kim, you can't just assume what someone else is feeling. Before you come down too hard on Ruth, I think you need to understand something about the different levels of a relationship."

I could tell Dad was about to launch into a lecture. Yet I wanted to hear what he was going to say.

"The first level of relationship," he was saying, "the most basic one for Christians, is the one between you and God. That's central, but not exactly what we're talking about here.

"A second kind of relationship yields itself to others. It's the 'I-help-you-because-God-helps-me' relationship. It banks on the idea that the other person can't repay the kindness, nor reciprocate the help. The giver receives personal satisfaction from giving, so also benefits.

"The third level of relationship is very special and rare. It is a friendship that is equally felt between both friends. Usually it begins and progresses easily and naturally, and the risk is taken for greater intimacy, deeper friendship. It usually grows between two people with similar goals and values, and similar lives.

"Ruth, I think, is operating on the second level, and you are trying to operate on the third. Both levels represent true friendship, and this is where the frustration comes in. I do not question Ruth's love for you or your love for her. But you are both simply experiencing friendship on two different levels."

Dad's words gave me a lot to think about. If I was honest with myself, I had to admit something: Maybe I'd been trying to force level-three relationships out of people when I was sometimes afraid to invest myself in giving level-two relationships.

Even as I wrestled with the implications of these thoughts, my mind became more settled and it got easier to relate to Ruth's feelings.

—Kim Ballard

WILL'S NEW HABIT OF WEARING BOWLING SHOES TO SCHOOL WAS HAVING A NEGATIVE EFFECT ON HIS SOCIAL LIFE.

PART TWO

GETTING STARTED

3. *Making Friends Takes Confidence*

Chris: Throughout high school and a good deal of college, I wasn't very pleased with the stuff that made me, me. I felt that I had a lot to complain about: My height (too short); my skin (too pale); my intelligence (too average); my athletic ability (too awkward).

I'm not saying that I didn't have friends because of these self-inflicted negative feelings. Yet I tried, tested, and at times exhausted the patience of my friends. I remember one very pretty blonde shouting at me in exasperation: "Why do you do that to yourself! Why do you always put yourself down! I get sick of hearing it!"

Which, of course, made me feel worse about myself.

Then I met Tom. I was a college sophomore at the time. Tom was a full-time staff member with a Christian group on campus. Since we were both Christians, and had developed a pretty good friendship, we spent time going around the dorms talking to guys about our faith.

One time we were in a student's room, and I had just finished telling him why I chose to become a Christian. As Tom and I got up to leave, this guy pulled out a chemistry book and griped about the toughness of his current assignment. I shook my head and said, "Don't ask me for help. I've always been pretty dumb in that subject."

Tom was unusually quiet as we left. When we slipped into the bucket seats of his old Cutlass, he threw back his forearm and landed a hard blow to my chest. Once he had my attention, and once I caught my breath (he was a pretty strong guy), he said matter-of-factly, "I never want to hear you say that again."

Immediately aware of what he was talking about, I responded, "Yeah . . . but I was always pretty good at English Lit." He smiled.

Tom and I spent most of that afternoon cruising campus, the convertible top of the Cutlass down, discussing the ways I put my self-concept through the shredder. I confessed that my self-esteem was not in good shape. I remember saying that I often lacked the confidence it takes to begin relationships. I promised to look for things in my life that were positives—things I was proud of.

Great awakenings don't always come by way of dramatic experience. Or by a sharp smack on the chest. In my case, Tom and other friends spent a lot of time encouraging me and showing faith in me. Learning to love myself has taken much time and much help from my friends. I have changed a lot since that day, but the change has come in many small steps.

A healthier self-esteem has undoubtedly helped my ability to make friends. Having more confidence in myself, I find it easier to reach out and befriend others. As a matter of fact, I am often complimented for being the first person to introduce myself to new people in a crowd.

Most people, like me, find that they can befriend others only as they learn to be friends with themselves. It's a long-term struggle that author Tim Stafford knows quite well. In the following story, Tim presents his personal battle for self-acceptance, and offers practical insights for all of us. His thoughts on befriending yourself lay a strong foundation for making good, lasting friendships.

CHAPTER 4.
Becoming Your Own Best Friend

I have scars tracing my cheeks in a coarse pebble grain. Bumps and dents mark where little red, pussy sores ran. Pimples leave scars.

But the scars on my face aren't the worst of it. They're so slight I can explore them with my fingertips and not feel them. I seldom think of them. The invisible scars on my mind, from shyness exaggerated by acne, are the most tender. Social illnesses leave scars inside.

Meeting strangers was always pure terror to me. When I was 12 I had a job as a paperboy. I liked the solitary early mornings on my bike, cutting corners just right, leaning backward to blindly clutch a paper and then heaving it on the way toward someone's porch, perhaps throwing a curve around a post, or angling the paper so it slid neatly 10 feet to the doormat. What I hated was collecting money once a month. I would put it off as long as I could, then slink from door to door saying as little as possible, hoping as I approached each door that no one would be home. What should have been the best part of the work—the payoff— was the worst.

The day before school pictures were taken, I might spend an hour in front of the mirror, finding just the right smile and then trying to memorize how it felt on my face. I never succeeded.

On top of the shyness came pimples, bursting on me at

age 14 like facial volcanoes. I was shy and doubtful enough about myself already. Acne confirmed my suspicion that I was ugly. No one could tell me it "didn't look bad." I'd know they were lying. A dermatologist told me the only helpful thing. "It's not your fault, you know," he said. He pointed at my father, who had brought me. "Blame him. Your parents gave you those genes, and now you have to live with them." Still, I blamed myself.

Friendship Never Occurred to Me

At lunch, clutching my tray, I would scan the cafeteria for familiar faces, always afraid of being left outside some protective cluster. It never occurred to me that everyone else felt the same way; it never occurred to me that I could strike out and become aggressively friendly. I only looked for protection and anonymity, the moment when a group parted slightly to accept me in and then closed around me without a ripple in the conversation.

I wouldn't be truthful if I left an impression of myself as a social misfit—one of those miserable few in every school who wander the halls, friendless. I was better off than most. I played sports, and I was a charter member of the elite crowd who ran the literary magazine. I had a girlfriend. I could carry on a conversation with even the most popular kids.

I had a good disguise for my weaknesses—cynicism. I am sure that I came across as self-confident, impenetrable, and arrogant. In some ways it was this disguise that scarred me most. Shyness makes us look vulnerable, hence very attractive; overcoming shyness can drive you to learn how to make other people comfortable. But covering shyness with cynicism, protecting it in a small band of sarcastic friends, keeps the self-hatred and the loneliness trapped inside. Wounds that should have stayed on the skin cut to the soul.

Wounds heal, of course. Just to write all this down would have been impossible a few years ago. The scab has fallen off the wound; the scars are fading imperceptibly to white, like old jeans. Something has happened. I have outgrown the acne, and more: I have outgrown the fears and self-hatred.

I explore my history through faded pictures of friendships and experiences. But I look in vain for a miracle. Something has happened to set me free, but what? No flash of insight revolutionized my mind; no friend in a single conversation healed me of all self-doubt; God did not startle me in the wilderness of my own bad feelings. Whatever has happened has come gradually.

So I'm tempted to prescribe what parents sometimes laughingly do: "Wait. Give it time. Your problems will go away." Will time cure a social illness?

I'm reminded of Ruth, whose problems don't go away. Ruth is beautiful in every way: She's smart, people like her, and physically she's perfect. You can look in her blue eyes and think how lovely it might be to be like her. But you'd better not look too deeply. Somewhere inside is a thick clot of self-loathing she can't cough up. Some social illness—I don't know what it was—left her mind paralyzed at the point of thinking herself worthless.

And I'm reminded of Johnny, who seems so hard and so smart. He's never given up that hardness; as a disguise for his fears, it's hardened into a permanent mask. Nothing has softened it. Nothing now seems to penetrate it.

Time does not heal all wounds. Something has to happen.

Letting Myself Be Loved

Again I explore my past, trying to find what made the difference. Was it some self-help trick, a positive mental attitude, or a formula for making friends? No. All I find are a few strings running through all those years. And all the strings are made of one substance: love.

What happened was this: someone loved me.

It is such a simple thing that we take it for granted. But I'm believing more and more that, in putting love before anything else, Jesus showed extraordinary wisdom. Love changes lives. You do not need a degree in psychology to use it. You do not have to thoroughly understand someone's problems. Love adapts itself to many circumstances and translates into any language.

Someone loved me. That has made all the difference and is still making all the difference.

Of course, you don't have to let love affect you. You can close yourself to it, from pride. You have to let yourself be loved. In all the changes that have come and are coming still, that is the only credit I can claim: I let it happen.

I let my family love me. In my case it wasn't hard, because there was good communication all along. Love and acceptance were always there. I know that's not true in many families.

Still, I know people who consistently pass up the opportunities that do exist. They pretend their family is irrelevant to who they are, cutting themselves off by always being too busy to try to hear the love between the lines.

I doubt you can ever really understand yourself apart from your family. And I doubt there are many parents who really do not love their children. Many don't express the love well: They express it by nagging or threatening or buying things for you. But the love is there, and you have to let it touch you. Otherwise it can never heal you.

I let my friends love me. Perhaps the most significant thing I ever did was to find friends who loved. Sometimes people who feel sorry for themselves look for friends who will make up for their deficits by being good-looking or popular or fun to be with. Tactically, it's a mistake, because those are the kids least in need of friends. But the biggest problem is simply that, as friends, they may not be worth much.

The friends who have mattered most to me have not been the most talented or the best-looking or the smartest. They have been good at caring for me. Time after time I was able to break out of my shell because they took the initiative. I could probably have had friends in a more admired circle. But I could hardly have found a more caring circle. I let them care for me. I let down barriers that would have kept them at a distance. I let them know me.

I let God love me. Of course, he already did. But I had to let him into my life; not just once, but many times. His love is not always easy to take. Sometimes it hurts to be loved, and it always hurts the pride. ("I don't need anything," we say, and kill ourselves.) I let myself believe what he said: that my performance didn't matter to him, but only the openness of my heart. There were plenty of opportunities to discard him and let his love slip quietly out of my life.

I let myself love myself. That may sound strange, as though there are two "me's." But there seem to be two sides to each of us: With one side we want to love ourselves, recognizing the good God has planted in us, and yet the other side wants to drown that love in dissatisfaction. We can focus on what we do right and can look for more opportunities to do it, or we can focus on what we do wrong and refuse to break out of the negative pattern we're in.

I looked for good to happen. I became convinced that God was using time to make me better and that I could look into the future with positive expectations. I expected to see good blossoming in my life.

So I took chances. I reached out to others, overcoming my fear of meeting people. It was hard and painful, and it would have been nicer to sit home and nurse my sorrows, but instead I kept trying to enter the worlds other people lived in. The more I did, the easier it became. The easier it became, the easier loving myself became.

You, Too, Can Find the Cure

To get cured you have to go to the doctor, and then to the drugstore, and you have to remember to take your medicine regularly. I put myself in a position to be "cured." I got close to those who loved me, and I let down my defenses to their love. And I began to love back actively. I got close to God, close to my family, close to friends who really cared.

I took action, but my action only made room for the love

that gave the cure. Love, which we take for granted in posters and greeting cards, which we use to sign our letters, which is the most common reaction to our first entrance in the world as tiny, ugly, helpless creatures—this ordinary thing is what we need to cure the crippling disease of self-hate. Love is around us: in our families, in our friends, in God, and in ourselves. But we have to let it in.

—Tim Stafford

CHAPTER 5.

Making Those Initial Contacts

Chris: A long, lonely hallway set the scene for my own struggle to find new friends. I was a sophomore at the time and I had just started high school. I remember walking down that corridor, alone. Classes were in progress, so no one else was anywhere around. My footsteps echoed loudly and I could see my fuzzy reflection in the newly polished tile floor.

I attempted to sort through all the changes and newness of my surroundings. How would I ever learn my way around? What would my classes be like? But foremost in my mind were questions of friendship: Will any of my old ninth-grade friends be in any of my classes? Will all the upperclassmen think I'm a jerk? Will I be able to make new friends?

Then I found my classroom and dropped my hall pass on the teacher's desk. I recognized several faces, but none of my close friends seemed to be in the room. Even those I recognized were somehow changed. The summer months had stretched out their heights, and put coarse shadows on the faces of most of the guys. I felt surrounded by strangers. As I slid into my seat, I knew my hard search for friends would have to start all over again.

As the early weeks of that new school year passed slowly, I felt alone—even when the hallway was jammed with students. Sometimes it was frustrating to watch other kids group up, while I stood off by myself. I remember weekends when I'd sit home all by myself. Or I'd drop by the local fast-food restaurants and see groups of kids joking and having a good time. For the longest time I just spent Friday and Saturday nights alone—watching at a distance while others enjoyed friendship.

Then I realized that I had to stop moping around. I had to get out there and give friendship a chance. And I had to do it by myself—stop waiting for others to make the first move. Yet my decision to be "more outgoing" wasn't an easy one. I'd spent far too long feeling sorry for myself and withdrawing. I had a lot of "relearning" to do. Most of all, I had to realize that there were people out there who wanted to be my friend—who needed my friendship.

True, there were several painful failures. I'd get into a conversation with someone and think, *Here's a guy I can hit it off with.* But the next time I'd try, he'd walk away or ignore me.

I also felt held back by "social standards." Since I didn't drink alcohol, I often became the odd man out.

Yet amid failure, friendship slowly happened. I remember playing a certain rock tune for a psychology project, and having Dan come up and say, "I didn't know you liked that group. I do too." That first conversation with Dan led to many more conversations, and a close, long-term friendship.

Then there was Kathy, who sat behind me in government class. By turning around and talking to her before and after class, I got to know her as a good friend. In fact, I even shared some of my poetry with her—writings that were so personal I had never shared them with anyone else.

There were others. John, for instance. I met him simply because he drove an old VW that was a lot like my own car. Our initial discussions about cars turned into longer talks about girls, music, and even our faith in God. John's friendship, which started on a pretty superficial level,

ERSKINE

became one of my best and most memorable high-school relationships.

All this is to say that lasting relationships often grow out of the little things we do to get to know others. Yet I must—we all must—be willing to take a chance at friendship.

A Plan of Action

Getting to know people doesn't just happen. Each of us must decide to take steps to make those crucial "first contacts." Here are some ideas I've pulled from my own experiences:

Look in the right places. Don't overlook the obvious. Light conversations with the person who sits in front of you

real and fake smiles

in history class may gain you a good and lasting friend. A stranger in the lunch line might become a friend to sit with during mealtimes.

Yet you will also want to seek out people with common interests. For example, during high school I had a strong interest in conservation and ecology. So I started the school's first Ecology Club and gained many friends who shared my interest.

You may not want to start a club, but you could do the next best thing. If you enjoy music, get involved in the school's music program, or join a local ensemble group or rock band. If you enjoy water sports, spend time at the Y getting to know fellow swimmers. And if you want to become a doctor, you may find someone with a similar goal volunteering at the local hospital.

Make the first move. Don't be afraid to be aggressive. I realize that this is not easy. Starting conversations with strangers or joining in a group sport has always been scary for me. But it has paid off in friendship.

Be friendly. Say hello. Smile. Show interest in what this person is doing. Basically, treat him or her as you'd like to be treated.

Take the time. Avoid asking questions that you don't have the time or willingness to hear the answers to. Don't rush the conversation, either. If you're in a hurry and seem abrupt, people get the wrong impression.

Remember names. When you initially meet someone, make the effort to remember her name and use it occasionally in the conversation. If she doesn't have to repeat her name, she'll know you were listening closely.

Listen. Make eye contact when someone is talking to you. Ask questions and wait patiently for a response.

Pay attention to the little things. When listening, keep in mind key things this person tells you about himself. When your paths cross again, you can refer back to that earlier conversation. In doing so, the person will realize that not only were you listening, but you cared enough to remember what he said.

Say a good word. People like to be (sincerely) complimented. Find something good to say about your new friend—and say it.

Laugh. A good sense of humor goes a long way in building a solid friendship.

Respect a person's space. Everybody needs time for themselves or for other friends. If you're always waiting at her locker, or always shoving your way behind him in the lunch line, you'll quickly wear out your welcome.

Open up slowly. Initially, stick with talking about everyday stuff—the weather, homework, the putty your lunchroom calls mashed potatoes. Deeper conversations will come naturally as a closer friendship develops.

Stick to the facts and be yourself. To feel like "one of the gang," I've often been tempted to stretch the truth a bit: to say I like a rock band I've never even heard of, or to say I want to go out and party when I really don't. If I did that, I would undermine my credibility. If I continually projected a false image, I'd eventually be known as "nothing but a fake." Stick to your beliefs. In the long run, doing so will pay off in real friendships.

Show a genuine interest in those you wish to befriend. People like people who are friendly—who show an interest in them and in their lives.

Here's an example. My friend Megan has a friend named Amanda. Amanda writes poetry that is actually a little strange. Yet Amanda's poetry is really important to her, so Megan takes the time to read what her friend writes. And as a result of Megan's thoughtfulness and interest, the friendship has grown.

Appreciate friends for who they are. If you want to gain new friends, don't like people for what you can "get out of" a relationship with them. People can sense when they're being used. They can also sense when they are being genuinely loved. And it is through "no strings attached" caring that you will gain lasting friendships.

Keep confidences. As a friendship develops, it may be tempting to tell others something your new friend said in secret. That's gossip. Don't do it.

Remember special times. Send a card on his birthday, give her a note of congratulations when she aces a tough test, show up at your new friend's soccer game. Special days and events mean a lot to a friend—and your interest shows just how much you care.

Be willing to expand your friendship borders. There are plenty of people out there who are dying to be your friend. No kidding. Look around. There are a lot of lonely people at your school. Don't ignore them as potential friends. Here's something my good friend Jim Long has said:

"Ask yourself: What does a person have to do to qualify for my friendship? If the standard is sky-high, lower it. Which is another way of saying: Don't be too selective.

"There is a place, of course, for being quite picky. If you

can find no common ground for beliefs and values, friendship will be a struggle. On the other hand, don't be too hemmed in by differences. Race, social groups, even religion too often become barriers to understanding. It is enriching and constructive to have friendships that cut across such 'uncrossable' boundaries.

"Be willing to befriend people without giving them a shopping list of changes they must make. Tolerate, even celebrate, the differences in others."

Finally, don't get discouraged. True, I have spent many lonely nights wishing for friendships. I have also gone out and attempted to make new friends. Sometimes my efforts have worked. Other times they have failed. But one thing I will never do is give up—because I know somebody out there needs my friendship.

.

"All I know is some guy in a white coat said there would be free flies if I brought my friends."

PART THREE

HOW TO MAKE FRIENDSHIPS LAST

The Positive Power of Talking— and Listening

6.

I'd only recently been transferred to Mandeville High, and was still meeting new people every day. But being a military brat who's moved many times, I'd grown accustomed to this ritual. Making new friends and adjusting quickly had become natural to me.

Except for one thing: Whenever I began to settle into some great friendships, my dad would get transferred and I'd have to move again. I rarely had the chance to develop closer friends.

I knew that a good relationship required lots of time. And I had always sensed a certain "chemistry" between two people who had a special friendship. But I had never experienced that kind of friendship myself.

Then I met Suzy.

I don't remember how we actually met. Her face and name were one of the many I had quickly memorized in the process of settling into my new surroundings. Ours was kind of an "acquaintance" friendship; a little past the I-know-your-name-and-you-know-mine relationship, but not much. I always thought Suzy was nice. We were both fairly new to Mandeville. We were both Christians, and we both went to a Baptist church.

We first got to really know each other, though, at a summer camp in South Carolina, where my church youth group had decided to spend a week. Suzy and her roommate stayed in the room next to mine.

Shortly after camp started, I found out that Suzy and I had signed up for the same vocal class, so we decided to walk together across camp to the chorus room. After chorus we ate lunch together, talking and laughing and having a good time. I had never known how much fun she was to be around.

Almost unexpectedly, we found ourselves together a lot that week. And we always had a great time. In just a matter of days, Suzy and I began to pair up wherever we went. We seemed to have that "chemistry" I had always imagined.

It was amazing how much we were alike. We agreed on everything from guys to food to music. I giggled at the lunch table one day as I discovered that I was not the only person on earth who put mustard on her french fries.

That week we gabbed nonstop—about ourselves, other people, college, just about everything. We especially talked about God. Both of us had been Christians for several years, and we soon discovered that we each wanted to be more consistent with our Christian faith. After sharing about God's place in our lives one evening, we prayed together, asking him to strengthen our commitment and help us live to please him.

That night became very special to me. It felt like the start of something new for Suzy and me—a unique Christian bonding that drew us even closer. For the first time I had found a close relationship, a special friendship with a future.

Time seemed to fly for the rest of the week at camp.

Once back home, there wasn't a day Suzy and I could not be found together. We arranged to take weekly voice lessons together in the nearby town of Covington. We went out for pizza, lay out at the pool, and just bummed around. Since stores and friends and things to do are so spread out in our area, we had to drive everywhere, so Suzy and I often talked in my green-M&M-colored Fiat as we drove.

The Campus Life Guide

I marveled at how much I opened up to her. I felt no need to hide my feelings or opinions; the "me" in me just flowed freely, without hesitation. And she liked it. "Just trust me, Mitch," she said. "And I'll trust you. A friend is one who knows all about you and loves you just the same." I knew strong relationships take time to develop; I wanted to invest all that was needed in my growing friendship with Suzy.

Too Busy for Friendship

The start of school in late August (Suzy's senior year and my junior year) immediately halted our lazy summer schedule. I wasn't prepared for school's effect on our friendship. We both submerged ourselves in extracurricular activities, as in previous years. In no time our schedules were clogged with Student Council meetings, halftime-show practices, and constant homework. There was always something going on. Every day was go here, do this, say that. Life was rush, rush, rush.

At first I didn't notice any change. But gradually, our once-frequent phone calls became more sporadic. We talked only between classes, and the late bell always cut the conversation short. Meetings claimed most of our lunch periods. Suzy hung around with her group of senior friends, and I with my junior gang. We began to see a lot less of each other.

Things eventually got so hectic that I would see Suzy only at our weekly voice lesson.

One day at school, when I was lounging in "The Pit" with a few of my friends, it hit me how far apart Suzy and I had grown. I saw her laughing with her friends on the other side and caught her eye for a moment. I thought, *Here we are, both having fun, but why don't we ever have fun together anymore?* A few minutes later she came up to me and said, "Hey, Michele, I'm sorry, but I won't be able to make it to voice this week. Catch you next week, OK?"

"Uh, OK," I managed, as she scurried off to her next class. What was happening? I wondered. Couldn't we find time from our busy schedules to share with each other once in a while? Then I thought, *I knew it wouldn't last.*

At first I tried to forget it. Blow it off, I told myself. You had fun this summer, now it's time to get back to the old life-style. Maybe you just don't have time to work on a close relationship. I wondered if I should go back to where I had started: forever maintaining shallow acquaintances and drowning my loneliness in a hundred school activities. At least I wouldn't get hurt that way.

But I also thought about sitting down with Suzy and talking about my feelings. As soon as I mentally rehearsed our conversation, however, fear swept over me. Suppose she tells me she had fun this summer, but is too busy now for a close relationship? Speaking up to her would put me in a very vulnerable position.

Still, I knew Suzy and I had experienced that certain chemistry over the summer. Our friendship had been real. I had to find out if she still wanted it. If that meant risking rejection, I'd have to take the chance.

A Friendship Preserved

One night I took her aside after a Campus Life club meeting. "Suzy," I said, my voice quivering, "when we became such close friends this summer, it was one of the best things that ever happened to me. I've never had a friend like you. But now we've gotten so involved in our school schedules, I feel like our relationship has died."

Suzy looked at me intently as I spoke, but said nothing. I went on.

"I'm not blaming either one of us, Suzy. But I want that same close friendship to continue during the school year, too. And if you don't want it, I need to know."

There, I've said it. I've laid my feelings on the line, I thought. Taking a deep breath, I braced myself for the worst.

She put her hand on my shoulder. "Oh, Mitch," she said, using my favorite nickname, "I've noticed what's been going

on. It's been bothering me, too, and I feel terrible that I haven't done anything about it. Let's see if we can work on spending more time together. We grew so close this summer, and now I consider you my best friend." Tears rolled down my cheeks as she spoke. I couldn't believe what I was hearing.

—Michele Buc

7.

Taking the Time to (Really) Listen

I have been thinking a lot lately about listening. Really listening. Different circumstances have triggered this new fascination of mine with hearing from the heart.

A close friend of mine ran into a mutual acquaintance. They exchanged casual greetings on the run. The entire conversation, as my friend related it to me, went like this:

"Hi, Don!"

"Fine, thank you. How are you?"

My friend was puzzled.

Also, I stepped into the local McDonald's at noon. The usual menagerie: A number of young mothers with small, loud toddlers. A smattering of workmen on lunch break. A few "suits." And a battalion of escaped students, savoring fleeting minutes away from North High School.

Where to sit? Not too many options. The suits look boring. The toddlers are loud. "Oh, pardon me, is that your foot?" Hard to maneuver through the masses with this tray. Ah, here. . . .

I took a seat adjacent to a table of . . . well, I'd guess them to be sophomores, munching Macs, fries—the usual. I noticed immediately that one voice rose above all the others.

"And so I just told my mother, 'Don't you understand? I have to. . . .'"

Wonder what that's all about? I blocked out the distracting voice, pried open the salad, wrestled the packet of vinaigrette dressing into submission, sipped Diet Coke.

Again, the same voice: "You simply would not believe how Jeff reacted when I told him. . . ."

And so lunch went, basically uneventful. Well, one of the employees dropped a tray of salads. Otherwise, a typical fast-food break. But I continued noticing this sophomore girl at the adjoining table—talk, talk, talk—and I quickly realized: While her vocal cords were racing, her friends' were idling. They grunted assent. They lazily acknowledged her stories with burger-chomping nods. But they did not talk. They listened. And listened. And listened. And . . . left.

Confession, they say, is good for the soul.

At one point I was greatly tempted to say to her, "Would you mind resting your voice for a while?" Or to them, "Didn't your mothers teach you guys how to talk?"

Perhaps you have had similar experiences. One person has such a monopoly on the conversation that you want to sell your property to the bank and drop out of the game.

Or maybe it works the other way with you. Maybe you have gotten home after a party and told yourself: "Motor-mouth, you talked the whole evening! You didn't allow your friends one word!"

Learning the Fine Art of Listening

Listening is a skill. Truly listening.

The heart kind of listening.

Simple silence—swallowing burgers and nodding—is not necessarily listening.

And certainly, nonstop talking is not listening.

So, what is listening?

And why bother learning the skill?

There is great power in listening. You can achieve more through simply listening than you might imagine. Far more than through nonstop talk. Even if the talk is clever and good.

A (Real) Friend Takes Time to (Really) Listen

I faced something quite sad earlier this year. It involved death. But I will spare you the gruesome details.

I was depressed.

I was angry.

I wanted to talk about what had happened and I wanted to forget about what had happened simultaneously.

Maybe you understand how that feels. But for now, the fact that I was having a rough time is not as important as what I want you to know about one friend's wise listening.

"Hi, Jim. Have lunch plans?"

"Not yet."

"Wanna get a hot dog at Wendy's?"

Briefly, here's what followed: We walked a few blocks to the other fast-food place. We made small talk. Exchanged stupid jokes. Waited in a long line. Ordered lunch. Talked. Ate. Talked. And retraced the few blocks to where we began. All within an hour.

My friend did not prospect for gems of gossip. He did not dig for morbid details.

He did make me feel free to talk. So I talked.

And he listened.

With his ears, sure.

But also with his eyes. (I knew I was being heard, I could see it.)

My friend also listened with his mouth.

By keeping it closed.

By using it wisely.

At times in the conversation, he let me know he was following me. He asked an appropriate question, he summarized what he thought I was saying, he expressed concern. But let me stress: He let me spend my words extravagantly, but he was a miser with his own.

Now, I don't think my friend took classes in listening—Utilizing Ears 101. He was simply being himself. Unselfishly.

I must tell you what it did for me to be heard. It released bottled-up frustration. (No, I was not blubbering, though I was upset. And my guess is that it would have been OK even if my emotions had been loose and flapping around.) Being heard carved the problems down to more manageable proportions. (Have you had that experience?) The hurt did not go away, but my talking and my friend's listening combined to remove much of its sting.

Five Traits of Active Listening

So, I have been thinking a lot lately about listening. Really listening. What it does and does not mean to disengage the mouth and activate the ears. Here are a few of my thoughts on what it means to hear with the heart.

This style of listening is tolerant. It is nonjudgmental. Even sympathetic. I may say something you do not agree with. I may be opinionated. The time may come for you to openly and clearly disagree with me. But listening means first hearing me out.

Have you noticed that there are some people who weigh ideas silently, in their minds, and only with great reluctance voice them? Other people shape ideas by speaking them aloud; they talk their way to a conclusion.

The person who listens tolerantly allows for both kinds of people. The tolerant listener accepts that he needn't be the critic, the judge, the corrector of the talker's ideas.

Listening puts effort into hearing feelings. It looks for clues in the talker's eyes, in the inflection of voice, in posture (a slouch, a shrug, a gesture, a smile, a tear).

Here's a similar but different thought:

Heart-listening is also perceptive listening. It looks beyond the words for clues to what the person really means. This listening scours the conversation in search of the talker's frame of reference. What experiences form the backdrop to this conversation?

People do not necessarily mean what they say. Words spoken, particularly under heated emotion, are often merely the shadow of true feelings, ideas, thoughts. If we are too quick to respond to what is being said, we may be spouting answers into a conversational mirage.

Listening that has power to help and heal is listening that is patient. It knows even nervous chatter is saying something; something about the talker's emotional needs, if nothing else.

And do you know how people recover from grief? Do you know how someone gets better after the pain of a divorce or a death? Several legitimate ideas could be suggested, but foremost is this: People talk themselves back to emotional strength. Something happens in the repetition of the story, in the repeated sharing of feelings, that may not happen as effectively in any other way. Can you patiently hear a friend's talk, even if the conversation is a rerun? Such patient hearing has astounding power.

Listening that works is, above all else, comfortable listening. The listener is not impatient, is not judgmental or easily shocked. The listener looks for clues as to what's behind the talk, and listens for feelings, not just words. All of that, but this too: Silence is not a conversational problem.

A friend of mine gave me his description of friendship: "I know someone is my friend when we can go on a long drive together without having to talk constantly. We are comfortable with silence."

Listening Says I Care about You

I don't want to be too critical of Don.

"Hi!"

"Fine, thank you."

We all have our times of absentminded preoccupation and out-of-sync responses.

Even burger-girl is understandable. Bubbly personalities often inadvertently over-sprizzle conversations.

But occasionally, at the time when we most need to be heard, true listening occurs. And when it does, something quite powerful happens. The person who listens, speaks. Speaks through the act of listening.

Listening says that you respect me. It tells me that you value me. It tells me that what I think and say is as important to you as what you think and say.

Your listening says that you love me. A friend told me about one of those psychological studies you read in textbooks. In this one, he said, faces were photographed with different expressions. Some were showing anger, others frustration, and so on. Then the pictures were displayed to people who were asked to identify what was happening in the photo—what was being expressed. Repeatedly, pictures of people listening with concern were mistaken for photos of people expressing love; the two were perceived as interchangeable.

I do not find that particularly surprising, though. Nothing says you care for me more deeply than when you simply listen.

—Jim Long

8.

The Little Things That Communicate Friendship

Kris: Talking and listening are essential to communication between friends, but there is a third element that communicates friendship: I call it "the little things." Sometimes we get so caught up in our own lives that we forget to reserve room in our schedules for our closest friends. But it is making time for "the little things"—meeting for lunch or a quick game of one-on-one, talking regularly, expressing appreciation for each other, catching a movie together— that keeps good friendships going strong even after you've been friends for a long time.

One of my forever friends, Stephanie, is an expert at maintaining friendships, because she remembers the little things. For example, she always pauses in the midst of her Christmas Eve activities to call me, long-distance, on my birthday. When I was in school, she'd come to my music concerts and my games. She sends me encouraging cards when I am having a difficult week. And this past spring, Stephanie took time out from her vacation to write me a letter that I'll always keep. She wrote just to remind me that she cares about me and that our friendship is important to her. I was struggling with some uncertainties she wasn't even aware of at the time. Her words really touched me.

The incredible thing is, Steph treats all of her close friends with the same sort of care. She knows that friendships don't "just happen." She works to make them work. Consequently, she builds lasting relationships.

Besides encouraging me, Stephanie's thoughtfulness influences me in two other ways. First, because she remembers me so often and makes time for our friendship, I naturally want to do the same for her. Giving back to her isn't a chore; I enjoy it.

The second result of Steph's efforts is that I end up feeling more secure about our friendship. We don't see each other every day—or even every month sometimes—but it's all right; I know she still cares because she frequently reminds me that she does. That security is important in all of my friendships.

Stephanie is a rare individual. Most people aren't as conscientious in their relationships. All of us can learn, though, to communicate care to our friends by planning some of these little things into our busy schedules:

Remember important dates and events. We've mentioned how recognizing birthdays and other special days can help deepen new friendships. They're just as important with old friends. Do you know what dates are special to your closest friends? Remember them with a card, a flower, or a note.

Attend important events. Be there for recitals, sports competitions, and other significant events.

Make a tape. Record your friend's favorite songs and give it to him/her.

Schedule time together. Agree on one evening a week or a month that is "your night" together, and use that time to relax, catch up, or play a game of tennis.

Arrange to pray together regularly. If you're both too busy to establish a time when you can meet for prayer, write out your prayer needs on index cards and hand them over to your friend at school.

Be spontaneous. At those times when you realize, "Hey, I really appreciate this person," tell him. Or write your friend

FRIENDSHIP MEANS "BEING THERE FOR EACH OTHER"

"My friend and I are always there for each other. If I'm down, he helps to boost my morale. I do the same for him."
                                    —Brian, Mt. View, California

"My best friend and I live miles apart. Yet we take the time to write each other often. Through letters we share our secrets and ask for advice. Writing isn't always easy, it takes a little extra time, but my friend is well worth the effort."
                    —David,
              Clearwater, Florida

"I have not drunk alcohol for three months straight. I really feel that I owe this to my friend, Sara. If not for her, I think I would still be drinking. She is a very special person—not once did Sara condemn me for the things I had been doing wrong. No matter how busy she is, she always takes time to listen. I love and respect her for that. She's made me see the good in myself and has helped me realize that it's good to be alive."
                          —Jill, Elkhart, Indiana

"Bob and I help each other a lot. Say he's got to do something around the house for his parents; I help him out. He does the same for me."
                          —Steve, Tampa, Florida

a quick note. Don't let those positive thoughts go by without sharing them.

Brainstorm fun things to do. Get together with your special friend or a group of friends, and dream up some fun: hikes at the local state park, a video night with a theme (old horror flicks, B-rated sci-fi movies, you name it), or throw a party where everyone dresses like his least favorite rock, movie, or TV stars.

"Listen, Margo! When I said I was glad we had a friendship where we could share everything . . . I wasn't talking about my boyfriend!"

PART FOUR

WHEN SOMETHING'S WRONG BETWEEN YOU

CHAPTER 9.

Confronting Problems

Kris: Criticism is about as popular as the common cold. Nobody wants to catch it. And we all politely try to avoid giving it to our friends. But there are times when the willingness to risk a word of sensitive, constructive criticism is a mark of real friendship.

When I think about the "constructive" side of criticism, my friend Kelley comes to mind. As a college freshman I wasn't very good at expressing my feelings. A lot of the time I'd sit on them, keeping my mouth shut if a friend offended me in some way. I was afraid to confront people. But as Kelley and I spent more time together, her style of communicating—especially the way she confronted—influenced me.

Kelley was up-front about her feelings in a way I'd never seen before. She wasn't afraid to say, "Kris, I felt like you were insensitive in this situation, and it hurt me." Words like those were hard for me to hear. I got defensive, because I thought her confrontation meant she didn't care about me.

But I didn't walk away from her honesty because deep down I knew I needed to hear the truth about myself.

I watched as two of my college suitemates, who called themselves friends, let several small problems accumulate into a big one. They talked to other people about their frustrations, but not to each other. Then one day, all the hurts and offenses of the previous six months came pouring out in a flood of anger. Both friends were hurt. I don't think the wounds from that confrontation ever fully healed.

If I hadn't spent time with Kelley, I probably would have concluded that confrontation is bad, causing more problems than it solves. But I'd been learning from Kelley about the right way, the loving way to constructively criticize someone. And I knew that my suitemates had gone about it the wrong way.

Kelley once explained her views on confrontation. She told me, "I hope you realize that I never say anything to hurt you. I only confront you because I care. I don't want you being mad at me without telling me why either." Then it all made sense. If our friendship was important to us, we couldn't afford to have unresolved hurts.

Being honest with each other doesn't mean we just insensitively blurt out anything that comes to mind, or even that we talk every time the slightest irritation crops up. Irritations come and go in a minute sometimes, especially when one of us is having a bad day anyway. But if an irritation might hinder our friendship, we need to sit down and talk through it.

Here's what I've picked up about giving constructive criticism:

Talk in private. When we're with our friends, Kelley and I often jokingly say to each other, "You're really ticking me off." But if there is actually a problem, no one will be in the room except us. We won't humiliate each other by confronting when there are people around.

Keep it between you. We made a pact that if there was ever a hurt or a problem between us, we'd talk about it only to each other. That pact hasn't been broken, and it's kept us close. I know Kelley won't talk behind my back because she always comes straight to me.

Confront immediately. We can't always talk the moment something happens, but Kelley and I confront the minor problems as soon as we're alone together. That way, bad feelings don't get the chance to accumulate.

It was apparent to all of Leonard's friends that his first role in a school play was going to his head.

Stick to one complaint at a time. That helps us keep situations from being so complicated that we can't work through them. It also decreases my defensiveness at Kelley's words, because I don't walk away feeling like I can't do anything right.

Be willing to compliment, and not just criticize. This is one of the most useful things I've learned from Kelley. When she tells me, "You're a very responsible person; it's great that people can really count on you," before telling me, "but I worry because you overbook yourself too often," the compliment softens the confrontation so that I'm willing to hear it.

Object only to what a person can change. Kelley can't influence how I'll feel in response to a situation, but she can talk to me about what I do with those feelings. For example, if I get upset about something, it's appropriate for her to confront me about my tendency to back off from people— but not about being upset. I can't help that.

Don't raise your voice. Yelling at each other has never been a part of our confrontations. It's a matter of respect for each other's feelings.

Avoid making blanket statements. Kelley doesn't say to me, "You *always* do this . . ." or "You *never* help me with that. . . ." Those two words can do more to put a person on the defense than anything.

Ask before you accuse. Kelley is good about asking, "Why didn't you meet me for lunch as we agreed?" instead of assuming I stood her up just to make her mad.

Accept each other's "response style." I'm the type of person who, after being confronted, needs a chance to think about what's been said and sift through it. After I've had a little time, I can respond more clearly to a person's words. Kelley is just the opposite. She can hear me out, think it through immediately, and respond right away. Since she's learned that I need some time, Kelley will say what she needs to say, and then free me to respond when I'm ready.

Just as there are useful guidelines for giving criticism,

there are techniques for accepting it. I try to do the following when Kelley (or anyone else) confronts me:

Listen to the criticism. This is sometimes the most difficult thing to do, especially if I disagree with what she is saying. But I look directly at her. I let her know I hear what she's saying by nodding my head. I turn my body to her, and I keep my mouth closed.

Don't launch a counterattack. It only makes an unpleasant situation worse. If I criticize Kelley simply because she criticized me, then nothing will get resolved. Besides, I need to remember that as a true friend, she came to talk because she cares about me, not because she wants to hurt me.

Don't joke about it. Humor can be helpful, but only after you've shown that you really take the complaint seriously.

Don't exaggerate the complaint. If Kelley says she felt I talked too much in one instance, it doesn't mean she thinks I'm always talking. I don't need to defend myself against a charge that was never made in the first place.

Let the other person know you understand his or her complaint (whether you agree with it or not). At times I restate or paraphrase the criticism to accomplish this. And if Kelley makes a statement that is vague, I'll ask questions so we both are clear about the problem at hand.

Think about what's been said. Even if I don't feel the criticism was valid, I ask myself: What did Kelley say that was true? What do I need to work on?

I don't want it to sound like I naturally "took" to being confronted or to confronting others—I didn't. I still don't enjoy it. But sometimes it's necessary if you want to keep a good friendship going strong.

10. *The Art of Compromise*

Kris: Like communication and confrontation, compromise is an essential friendship skill. Yet when I think about compromise, here's what usually comes to mind: giving in to someone else's negative values, going along with a friend's bad ideas.

True, that's one side of compromise. However, there is a positive side. For example, there are times when it is good to "give in" in order to build a better relationship.

The hard part is in knowing when to and when not to compromise, for friendship's sake. Diane Eble offers these helpful guidelines:

When a Friend Needs You

Don was walking out the door to pick up Jim and go on to the game when the phone rang. "Don? Glad I caught you." It was Jim. "I—I just can't make it to the game today. Go on without me."

"What do you mean? This is a big game! We'll have a blast with everyone else there. What are you going to do with your ticket?" Don couldn't believe Jim was canceling out.

"Look, I just can't make it, OK? Something came up." Jim's voice sounded strange, kind of far away.

"Is everything OK? What's the matter?"

"It's nothing," Jim said. "I just don't want to go to the game today, that's all."

Something was wrong; Don knew it. Jim was a bigger baseball fan than he was, and wouldn't have backed out of going to see his favorite team just because he didn't feel like it.

Don felt torn. He had been looking forward to this game for a couple of months. And the tickets were pretty expensive. He wasn't sure he could find someone to buy his ticket at the last moment. Yet Jim was his best friend, and something was obviously bothering him. . . .

"Look, Jim," Don said, "we don't have to go to the game. I just wanted to do something fun with you today. How about if I pick you up and we go to the beach?"

"I guess so."

After a long swim, Jim finally told Don what was eating at him: His parents had just told him they were getting a divorce. Don listened as they sat on their towels, sweat and sand caking their skin. He thought of the unused ticket sitting on his desk at home. It seemed like a small thing compared to what Jim was going through.

Your Need Over My Desire

Sometimes friendship means compromise—positive compromise. We do it all the time, often without thinking about it. Your friend has a need. You give up something to meet that need, as Don did. You change your plans. You go out of your way to listen. You put the important need of your friend above your own valid, but less important, goal or desire.

Compromise Can Show Loyalty

Sometimes compromise is just another word for unselfishness. Consider Julie and Kim.

When Kim went out with Brett, Julie was secretly a little jealous because she liked Brett, too. A month after Brett broke up with Kim, he asked Julie for a date. She wanted to say yes, but she knew it would hurt Kim. She told Brett no—it wouldn't work. And she never told Kim that Brett had asked her out.

Compromise may mean you sacrifice something in order to meet your friend's expectations. Julie knew Kim expected her loyalty. And much as Julie would have liked to date Brett, it just didn't seem worth hurting Kim and possibly ruining a friendship.

At times you have to give up something you really want, because the friendship is just more important. Sometimes compromise is another word for loyalty.

Handling Differences of Opinion

Cindy and Pam were college roommates. They were fairly compatible in most areas—except for music. They had completely different tastes—and different ideas on how loud to play the stereo. Cindy liked to listen to heavy metal—full blast, of course. Pam enjoyed Christian pop (music Cindy couldn't stand).

It complicated matters that Pam liked to listen to music while she studied—and the stereo was hers, after all. She would automatically turn it to the local Christian radio station, or switch on a favorite tape whenever she entered the room. Cindy began to see this as a personal attack. The tension between them started to crackle.

Pam and Cindy were in danger of letting a difference in taste ruin an otherwise positive friendship. What should you do if you're in a similar situation, and you and a friend just can't agree on something?

Separate the person from the problem. Once Pam and Cindy realized that they simply had different tastes in music—and that neither's taste was any better or worse than the other's—they were able to see the real problem: They just didn't want to listen to each other's music. Agreeing that it's OK to disagree can free you to confront the heart of the issue.

Focus on interests, not positions. Rather than arguing about what kind of music each of them listened to, or when they listened to it, Pam and Cindy needed to discuss their true interests. When they did, they found they shared a lot.

They both wanted to be able to occasionally relax by listening to music they liked; both wanted to be able to concentrate when they studied, without distractions; both wanted to feel accepted by the other.

To identify their real interests, Pam and Cindy had to be honest. To avoid the trap of blaming the other person, they used "I-messages": Instead of saying, "You're so inconsiderate when you turn on your music while I'm studying," Cindy said, "When I study, I have to concentrate or I just can't follow things. When you turn your music on while I'm studying, I feel like you're not considering my needs or feelings at all. Can we work out a compromise?"

And they both had to try hard to listen and understand each other, to lay aside their own positions for a while and put themselves in the other person's shoes. To try to hear the feelings behind the actual words. To mirror back what they heard their friend saying: "In other words, you feel that when I play my music without asking you if it's OK first, it's like I'm ignoring you're even there?"

Once Pam and Cindy had clarified what they really wanted and felt, they were able to take the next step.

Invent ways to get what you both want. Cindy and Pam brainstormed ways to achieve their mutual interests: They could buy headphones; Cindy could purchase her own stereo and headphones; they could set up times when each would be free to listen to the music she wanted; both could agree to not make remarks about the other's music, etc. From these options they chose the solutions that seemed workable, and decided to try their plan for a month. Then they would discuss how it seemed to be working at month's end.

Not all disagreements with friends require such an elaborate plan of compromise. Sometimes all you have to do is give up a position. Better to lose an argument and keep a friend than to win an argument and lose a friend.

Sometimes compromise is another word for humility.

Compromise May Mean Tough Choices

Obviously, we can't ignore the negative side of compromise. Compromise can undermine the very friendships we want to preserve. Sometimes compromise is just another word for copping out. Here was Greg's dilemma.

The guys were at it again: They were talking about Mark and what a wimp he is. There were other words: fag, homo, queer. Stories flew around the locker room—stories that made Greg sick. Stories he knew weren't true. Greg knew Mark. Mark would call Greg a friend. So why couldn't Greg open his mouth and tell the guys to shut up, to leave Mark alone?

Because these guys were also Greg's friends, that's why. Friends he didn't want to turn against him. So he kept his mouth shut. As Greg walked out of the locker room, he wondered who was the real wimp. Maybe it was him, for not defending his friend Mark.

Whatever he did, Greg felt like he'd be a loser.

In such situations, how do you know what to do?

It helps to have a standard. The Bible, God's Book, offers some clear ones. For instance: "Let love and faithfulness never leave you; bind them around your neck, write them on the tablet of your heart. Then you will win favor and a good name in the sight of God and man" (Proverbs 3:3−4). If Greg had made his standard "love and faithfulness" toward his friends—not only Mark, but the guys in the locker room as well—what might he have done?

No doubt he would have defended Mark, saying something like, "Come on, guys, where did you hear that story? I know Mark, and he's really a pretty OK person." In saying this, he would obviously be showing loyalty to Mark. But, less obviously, he would also be showing faithfulness to his other friends. He would be saying, in effect, "I am loyal to my friends. I don't let people cut them down behind their backs. And, incidentally, the same would be true about you, too. If someone cut you down, I'd defend you."

Weighing Good and Bad Compromise

Karen and Tom were in fourth period study hall together. Tom had just taken a history test—the same test Karen was about to take in fifth period. As soon as they sat down in study hall, Karen leaned over to Tom and whispered, "OK, so what was the test like? What did Mr. Johnson ask?"

Tom felt uneasy. He hedged. "I don't really remember the questions too well. There were a lot of them."

"Oh, come on, you must at least remember the essays. You know I studied, since we studied together. I don't see why you can't just give me an idea of what to focus on. I'd do the same for you, you know that," Karen added.

What could Tom say? He knew she would do the same for him. They were good friends. *Except I wouldn't ask*, he said to himself—then dismissed the thought. "Well, OK, just the essay part. There were four questions; we only had to answer two. . . ."

Sometimes we compromise standards for the sake of friendship. The relationship looms large, the standards seem somewhere in the distance. It happens a lot in romantic relationships. It happens at parties. It happens in any situation where the pressure of the moment fuels a natural tendency to avoid friction in a friendship: "Just this one time can't hurt. . . ." "Maybe I am being too rigid. . . ."

Friends have expectations of us. Sometimes those expectations are good, and they call out the best in us. But sometimes the expectations are not quite so noble. They're more selfish: "I expect you to give me what I want, regardless of whether it hurts you."

By asking Tom to tip her off concerning the test questions, Karen was placing her own desire for a good grade above her consideration for Tom's integrity. By giving in to Karen's expectation of help, Tom compromised a bit of his own honesty.

Sometimes Compromise Means Betrayal

Sometimes compromise is another word for betrayal. Betrayal of our own best interests and deeply held values. Betrayal of our commitment to follow what we know is best.

Bridget and Linda had been best friends since grade school. They hung out with the same crowd, too—one of the more popular crowds at school. But then Bridget became a Christian, and she began to feel uneasy about some things, particularly the drinking and the making out that went on at parties. She got around the drinking by offering to drive her friends home from the parties, telling everyone she didn't want to drink and drive. But sometimes, when the parties were in the neighborhood, she couldn't use that excuse. She'd have a wine cooler and then feel bad about herself.

Then Linda started pressuring Bridget to have some parties at her house, and Bridget didn't have a good excuse. She was getting tired of making excuses to Linda and the others. And she was tired of giving in and feeling bad about herself. For Bridget, compromise was beginning to feel like a trap. A trap she wasn't sure how to get out of.

When Your Friends Drag You Down

There are times when compromise is impossible. Or at least undesirable. When our friends are bringing us down— continually forcing us to choose between them and our own conscience—it's time to reevaluate. It's time to make some tough choices.

Bridget came to the painful realization that she and Linda didn't have much in common any more. Not interests (Linda wanted to party and drink; Bridget was beginning to get serious about grades and sports). Not morals (Linda openly admitted that she was sleeping with her boyfriend; Bridget had just broken up with her boyfriend because he was pressuring her).

But it was hard for Bridget to give up Linda. And hard for

The Campus Life Guide

her to give up her place in that crowd of friends. The only way she could do it, Bridget decided, was to find a new set of friends. People she could feel good about; people who shared her interests and values.

Bridget started to hang out more with kids from her church youth group. She also spent more time with people from her softball team. Then, when Linda would invite her to a party, she could truthfully say that she had other plans. Bridget did invite Linda to some of the youth group activities, but Linda kept putting down Christians.

Finally Bridget had to confront Linda. They talked for a long time. Bridget told Linda she still cared about her, but they didn't have much in common any more and probably couldn't be best friends. It was hard, but afterward Bridget knew she had done the right thing.

After that conversation, Bridget and Linda saw each other at school, but they weren't as close. For a few months not having a best friend was lonely for Bridget. But the relief of not having to make up excuses, of not feeling bad about what she was doing, outweighed the pain.

Sometimes compromise is another word for selling out. And that's just not worth it. Not even for a friend.

—Diane Eble

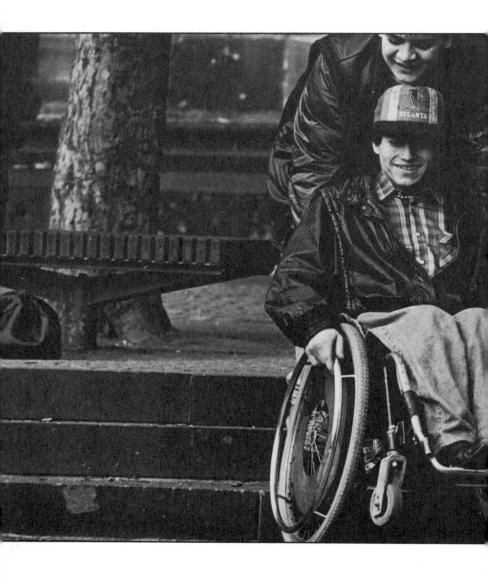

PART FIVE

HOW TO HELP A HURTING FRIEND

11. *Letter from a Friend*

Dear Jonathan,

I know it's strange to get a letter from someone you see almost every day, but I don't exactly know how to talk to you about this. So I decided to express myself in writing, because I think it may be easier to communicate how I'm feeling right now. I have trouble trying to vocalize my needs, but I do need you.

You don't know how much I'm hurting now. I can't believe my dad's dead, and that I'm never going to be able to see him again. Worse, since I've been here at school, 350 miles from home, it's hard to actually realize he's gone. I wonder if I've ever even admitted to myself that he's dead. I go on living my life, going to classes like everything's normal. Shouldn't I be sitting around in sackcloth and ashes, experiencing my grief, instead of pretending everything is OK?

I've had only one good cry, and that was about a week after his death. We had just watched a movie in one of my classes where someone died of cancer. I was kind of reliving my experience with Dad. I also cried because I wasn't there with him. I was supposed to have been there. We were sure it would work for me to fly home. We were sure we'd have more than a few hours' notice.

And then for the death to be so hard . . . hasn't enough happened to us? Couldn't God have, at least, been a little merciful and let Dad have a peaceful death—and let me be there with him, and with Mom and my sister?

I was supposed to have a chance to say good-bye to Dad also. When I left to come back to school after Christmas, I told him good-bye and said I loved him, but I was supposed to get a chance to really say good-bye to him for good. It's not fair. I wish Dad could still be here to see me graduate from college and start seminary. I was so close to finishing college—I hurried through in three years so that maybe he could see me graduate. You'd think God could have given us just five more months.

Since I've gotten back to school after Dad's funeral, nothing has been the same. I've been here for nearly a month now, and I can count on one hand how many people have mentioned the fact that Dad died, or even that I've had some pain in my life. Sure, people have said they're glad I'm back, but that's all. They even seem to be avoiding me. It's not fair. I'm at this Christian school, and no one will help me with my pain. Everyone's too busy with their own lives.

I understand it, but I wish that, at least once, someone would stop and talk to me about it. I want to talk about my pain and my father's death, and I want to be around people—but I don't have the opportunities. I even *need* to be around people. I need help dealing with all of this. I don't want to do it alone. I need someone who will listen and someone who will help me cry.

Why won't anyone cry with me?

Won't you please help me cry?

People avoid the subject of Dad's death when they are around me. I've had a few faculty members mention it to me and offer their sympathy, but some of the people I expected to say something haven't said anything.

Even the college chaplain hasn't said a word to me about Dad's death. I know he knows about it, because someone said he announced it in chapel while I was gone. He helped me a lot last year when I found Dad's leukemia had turned acute.

Lori told me that some people have asked her how I am. I wish they'd ask me, because a lot of times I want someone to talk to. I want someone to help me experience my pain and share it. I know I can't expect them to, but it would mean so much to me if they would.

It's as if I died myself. As if my friends have died to me. Being dead would be better than living alone.

It seems nobody has time for death. On our way to the cemetery after the funeral, cars were passing us, hurrying on their way. Ignoring our pain. People are still doing that. Most of my friends are doing that. They are hurrying on with their lives while my world has stopped, or at least slowed down considerably for a while. It's not fair that everyone else's world goes on. I need to stop and rest and cry for a while, but people won't let me. I need to cry, and I need your help to do so. Won't you please cry with me?

Mom has been lucky because she has such a circle of friends around her. There are many people from the church who are helping her. The pastors have been so good, but they're a state away from me now.

I don't mean to say it's any easier for Mom. She is alone now because my sister and I are both away at college. She has to go home to an empty house; she has to go to church alone; she has to go on alone. That's what is probably the most unfair thing of all. Why does my mom have to be a widow? Why does she have to be alone?

Sometimes I really feel guilty. A few months ago, Dad was getting a little better and I was mad. You see, we'd known for a little over a year that he was going to die eventually, and I wanted to be able to get on with the rest of my life.

How selfish can a person be? Yet I just couldn't stand any more of those ups and downs: He'd get better and then get really bad again. Sometimes I have to wonder if God isn't actually quite sadistic: He's up there, having a good time torturing us.

I'd like to talk to you or one of my other friends about this, but everyone is so religious that it would never work. They can't handle my talking about it. And considering their responses, I'm not sure if I'm still a Christian. Sometimes I wonder why I'm still planning on seminary next year. God doesn't seem to be doing much for me. But still I want to become a pastor.

It doesn't make sense. I know I believe intellectually that God loves me. I just can't believe it inside. There's too much that's gone wrong. Where is God? Why isn't he here with me? Or if he is here, why doesn't he make himself known?

I don't trust my faith anymore. I don't know if or what I believe about life after death anymore. Dad's gone now from me. I can't pray, either. I try, but I just can't do it. What kind of pastor am I going to be if I can't even pray?

I was hoping to get someone from my dorm floor to help me get back in touch with God. But I just can't bring myself to ask. I can't let them see me like this. I know I should ask, but I just can't. The people at school just don't understand. They talk about Jesus and how wonderful their lives are as Christians. They can't relate—and could never understand how I can claim to be a Christian and still doubt God, and not pray or read the Bible.

I am trying to get back to a good relationship with God, but we're not on speaking terms right now, so it's hard. If only you could reintroduce the two of us. It's not like God's given up on me, or that he's left me. I'm sure he's still here and still cares; it's just that I can't sense it now.

It's almost like I need to forgive God. I don't mean that he's done something wrong, but from my perspective, he could have done a lot of things better. Maybe if I forgive God we can go back to being friends.

I need so much to have someone here who cares. I hurt inside and I need to let it out somehow. I want to cry, but I can't. I want to cry. I want a hug so badly. Won't you please cry with me?

—David Baer

The Campus Life Guide

CHAPTER 12. *When a Friend Hurts*

Chris: David's letter to Jonathan is really about the two sides of pain and grief. First, there is the obvious side: David's. His deep feelings of loss are normal, and most likely will last a long, long time. It's also normal for David to feel abandoned and angry—angry at his friends, his chaplain, and God. His doubts about his faith are normal too. It's all a part of the grieving process.

Then there is Jonathan's side—the side of the caring (or uncaring) friend. How should Jonathan have responded to his friend's grief? Certainly, withdrawal from David wasn't the answer. That just compounded the hurt and added to David's loneliness. Pat answers also needed to be avoided. Easy solutions just don't work when a friend is experiencing so much intense, personal pain. What then should Jonathan have done? What should any of us do when a friend is hurting?

David answered that question with this question, "Won't you please cry with me?" He needed his friend to simply care for him, hug him, listen to him. To be silent, and listen.

It sounds right. But it's not always easy to do. If Jonathan could have written a response to David's letter, he might have said: "But how in the world do I keep from making mistakes? How do I do it right? I feel so awkward about this whole thing. I'm afraid I might say or do something wrong or stupid. I mean, if I smile, won't that make you feel worse?

And if I frown all the time, won't that drive your depression deeper? I don't know what in the world to do. . . . So I avoid you."

Let me get personal. Like many of us, I have played the role of Jonathan on a few occasions. One particular time comes readily to mind.

Karen called my dorm room one night. It was around 1:00 A.M. My groggy head cleared when she whispered, "Suicide." Since I knew her fairly well, I was aware that she had tried killing herself several times before. She had been in and out of counseling; I took her seriously.

At first, Karen's voice sounded extremely agitated and nervous. She did a good deal of the talking. She talked about her failures at school, her poor relationship with her parents, her terrible self-image. That's what she did for the first hour or so. She talked. She cried. I mostly listened.

Around 2:00 her words slowed; she grew more depressed. I started asking questions, probing some of the stuff she had said earlier. She answered each question, then seemed to be waiting for the next. I asked, she answered. I asked, she answered. That went on until about 3:00. At this point, the conversation turned to me. I told her about myself, my background. I told several stories, some of them humorous, about my high-school years. By around 4:30, she sounded more at ease. She even laughed a little. Eventually she said she was much better and thanked me for being there.

Before she hung up, I got her to promise to go over to the health clinic. She said she would. I gently put the receiver down, then fell back in my bed exhausted, drained, unable to sleep.

Later that morning I called a friend of Karen's. This friend said that Karen had gone over to the clinic and was now doing fine. I was relieved. And I felt pretty good about the conversation that took place between Karen and me. I felt like I might have kept her from another suicide attempt.

But then something happened. Not to Karen, but to me. I saw Karen a few days later, and I just didn't feel comfortable around her. Actually, I ignored her. No, Karen had never been the clingy type; I wasn't ignoring her because she would turn into a leech if I didn't. I just didn't know what to say or do. I simply didn't know how to act around her. When she needed a friend, a hug, or even a fairly innocuous "Hi! How are you?" I wasn't there.

Karen never called me again at 1:00 in the morning to discuss her pain, or at 1:00 in the afternoon to discuss classwork or boyfriend troubles. Because of my uncomfortable feelings, because I just didn't know what to say beyond what I'd already said that one night, I alienated her. It wasn't the right thing to do, but I didn't know what "the right thing to do" was.

Years later I have come to realize something. If I brush you off, pull away from your pain, you will find it extremely hard to forgive me. I have also discovered something else. It's not what I say that matters. It's simply important for me to be there. To be caring. To be a real friend. I'll never blow it with a hug or a simple hello. And even if I do say something stupid, you will forgive my ignorance. You'll just be glad to have me there.

CHAPTER 13.

Ten Practical Principles for Helping a Friend

The following principles for helping others were developed by psychologists. Whether your friend is grieving a death, suffering depression, or hurting from a less serious problem, these principles will guide you as you seek to reach out:

1. Lend an Ear

Psychologist Carl Rogers pioneered a whole field of psychotherapy based on listening. If you could peek into a session with Rogers, you'd see a highly trained physician with years of schooling nodding in agreement as his client talks. In all probability, the doctor could handle his client's problem with a few choice words of learned advice, gleaned from years of textbook cases. Instead he listens, because he knows that's what his client needs most.

It's not easy to be a good listener—we all like to talk. But when a friend is in trouble, he doesn't need to hear about your problems, or be told that others have it tougher than he does, or listen to some warmed-over advice on what you think he ought to do. People who are anxious, frightened, or depressed feel much better after talking about their feelings. Leave the psychoanalysis to a doctor, and the advice to Ann Landers. Just listen.

2. Lend a Hand

Sometimes problems are beyond words. At a funeral or in a hospital room, a concerned look and a gentle touch or a

FRIENDS HELPING FRIENDS

"After an eight-year struggle with bulimia, I shared my secret problem with my closest friend from church. I thought she would totally reject me when she found out. Instead, she unconditionally accepted me. As a matter of fact, she once suffered from the same problem; we began meeting often, and she has helped me a great deal."
  —Lisa, Mount Vernon, Washington

"My best friend and I have shared some very important moments. Those times have helped me quit drugs and saved me from a lot of other negative things. Yet those big, dramatic times are really just the 'flesh' of our relationship. The skeleton supporting them is made up of our day-to-day friendship: going out to lunch on Sunday afternoons, talking on the telephone for long hours about nothing and everything, a smile and a hello at school.

"By sharing our everyday lives together, we became one at heart, forming a bond of friendship and love that will keep us together long after college separates us."
  —Wally, Lompoc, California

"When my grandmother passed away, I called Jenny. She came over, and as soon as she saw me, she gave me a big hug and a shoulder to cry on. We talked that night until 3:00 A.M. I don't know what I would have done without her."

  —Jill, Hicksville, Ohio

hug can be worth more than any cheerful word you might say.

Scientists tell us that our body language is so sophisticated that it exceeds words. A baby will never develop well unless he's touched often, and adults need simple human contact also. Especially when someone feels lonely and alone, a reassuring touch can break down the walls of isolation. No words are needed.

3. Share Something to Eat

What's the first thing the Red Cross does at the scene of a disaster? They go to work serving hot coffee and sandwiches. Offering food does more than boost calories—it provides a sense of security and reassurance. It's no mystery that food and caring go together. From the crib, eating and love are closely associated in our minds.

Eating can also take care of the physical need created by a tragedy. Doctors know that sometimes a person in severe emotional stress—from grief, sorrow, or fright—will go into shock. A friend in shock may act dazed, confused, irrational, or hysterical because the blood-sugar level in his body has dropped severely. Eating brings the proper levels back into balance, and may bring your friend around.

You don't have to wait until someone's in shock to practice this step. Look around. Are there people in your own high-school cafeteria sitting alone? That could be a sign that they need help. You can start by eating lunch with them. It's a small thing, but it would mean a lot to people who are used to eating by themselves.

4. Offer Practical and Realistic Help

"Everything will be all right" sounds awfully glib to a friend who's failing algebra, or breaking up with a boyfriend, or whose parents are going through a divorce. Remarks meant to reassure can often have the reverse effect if the person suspects you're not sincere. A down-to-earth, realistic attitude is the most helpful. Avoid giving out pious platitudes or homey, sugar-coated sayings. Real help may cost something; it might mean real work. For example: Ron was losing his place on the football team due to low grades in history. Everyone he talked to said, "Don't worry, you'll make it." Everyone except Bill. When Ron told Bill he was scared of getting kicked off the team, Bill offered to help him study twice a week after practice. That practical help was just what Ron needed.

5. Remain Objective

Chances are, if your friend is a close one, you can't help getting caught up in his feelings. You empathize and sympathize with him. That's good. But in order to be a true helper, you also need to control your own feelings. For many people, finding partners in misery is easy; finding someone who can stay calm and objective enough to help work things out is more difficult. A case in point: Cindy had a weight problem, and Debbie—also overweight—thought she could help. "After all," she said, "who understands what you're going through better than I do?" But after several months of frustration, Debbie stopped trying to help—and their friendship fell apart. Cindy hadn't gotten the help she needed because Debbie was too close to the problem herself.

6. Don't Play Judge

"You should never have . . ."; "It's wrong to . . ."; "If I were you, I'd have done. . . ." Such statements rarely help. Assigning blame for the problem at hand may make you more comfortable, but it doesn't do much for your friend. Instead, try putting yourself in your friend's situation. How would you feel if you were experiencing what your friend is going through? "I'm sorry that happened to you" or "What can we do now to set things right?" are statements that siphon guilt away from the problem, and take you out of the judge's seat. Jesus, the greatest friend and counselor a person could have known, didn't take it upon himself to judge people who came for help. He offered compassion, strength, and understanding.

7. Don't Go Overboard

One problem a friend in a jam doesn't need is an over-anxious helper. We all know people who, the minute they hear of trouble, "saddle up their horse and ride off in all directions." Doesn't the following sound familiar?

Dave showed up a half-hour late for a movie with Mike. "I've been waiting for you," Mike said. "Is anything wrong?"

"Oh," Dave sighed, "Mr. Franks made me work late again tonight. We're not getting along too well these days."

"Maybe you should talk to him. Get it out in the open. Maybe you should start looking for a new job. I know they're hiring delivery boys at Pizza Palace. I'll call and see if the manager's in. We'll go over tonight."

"I'd rather just relax and forget it. Can we still make the movie?"

"I'm not going to stand by and let you do nothing! We're going to find you a new job right away."

"Well, see you later, Mike. I just remembered, I promised Dad I'd wash the dog. I'd better be going. Bye."

Many times people only want someone to talk with—not a complete takeover.

8. Know Your Limits

As much as you would like to save the whole world, it isn't possible. Some of your friends may have problems that are beyond your knowledge and experience. Getting deeply involved in a problem that is over your head could make you part of the problem rather than the solution. When setting out to help someone, acknowledge your own weaknesses and limitations. Don't promise more than you can accomplish—even in the little things. It's easy to say, "I'll come visit you in the hospital," and then forget all about it. A slip-up like that can make a big difference to someone who needs you.

Another danger is overextending yourself. You won't do anyone any good as a burned-out wreck. Helping someone takes time, energy, and stability on your part. If you can't offer those things 100 percent, it's best not to take on another person's problems.

9. Suggest Professional Help

Occasionally you'll have a friend who needs special care. If, after getting all the facts, you decide that you're in over your head, don't be afraid to suggest professional counseling. Psychologists and other professional helpers are usually available (many times they work in conjunction with local schools). If that seems too threatening to your friend, suggest he talk to a minister. Many clergy are trained in professional counseling techniques, yet are not as intimidating for some people to talk to.

You may want to ask around for a competent helper before suggesting anyone to your friend. Of course, anytime you act in a friend's behalf, it should be done in strictest confidence. Don't ruin hard-earned trust by blabbing the details of your friend's problem to everyone you come in contact with.

10. Pray for Your Friend

One thing Christians can do for their friends is to pray for them. "Prayer changes things" isn't simply a cliche. It's true. Consider: Ellen was having difficulty dealing with her parents. It seemed all they ever did was fight with her about every little thing. She mentioned her problems to Jim, who decided to pray for her every day. One day Jim got a call. It was Ellen. "You know, it's the strangest thing," she said, "but since I talked to you, I don't feel as restless anymore. And my parents have eased up on me."

Although it's mentioned last in this list, prayer should be the first thing you do.

Ernie's attempt to impress his friends with a triple gainer and combination jackknife dive didn't quite work.

PART SIX

WHAT IT'S LIKE TO BE BEST FRIENDS

14. *Making a Friend for Forever*

Kris: Carol is one of my best friends. One of the consistent memories we share is sitting across from each other at her parents' kitchen table, talking whole evenings away—but always with either burgers, pizza, or her homemade chocolate chip cookies in hand.

When I think of her, I think of dreams. Carol has had much to do with the fact that I'm writing today, because she encouraged me throughout high school and college: "Keep writing, Kris. I know you can become anything you dream, but you've got to believe it."

And I think of prayers: We have faithfully prayed each other through the past several years. These are the memories that make her one of my best friends.

Such friendship is something we strive for, and it is a worthy goal with its own special rewards. Because of this, Chris and I decided to give the topic a section by itself. We interviewed three different pairs of best friends—two guys, two girls, and a guy and a girl—to get their perspective on this wonderful form of friendship. Hopefully, our conversations with them will give you plenty of ideas for building your own long-lasting relationships.

15. *Todd and John*

The Makings of a Friendship?

As high-school students back in Shawnee, Kansas, Todd and John had a pit-bull kind of relationship. They'd get together with their church youth group and somebody (usually one or both of them) would organize a team sport. Maybe football. Then the intense rivalry would take over. John and Todd always became opposing team quarterbacks. It wasn't simply about winning "a game"; winning meant more friends and more status. Theirs was a personal battle fought out of envy and jealousy. Not the kind of stuff that builds a best friendship.

John: Todd loved to play soccer and I loved to play football. In Sunday school class we'd always have this big argument over which sport we'd play that afternoon. I would get pretty upset if people wanted to play soccer, because Todd has a real talent for the game and I don't. If everyone chose soccer, I felt they were siding with Todd and slamming me. For each of us it came down to this: Who would be the leader? Who would have the largest following?

We didn't just compete in sports, though. We competed for girls. . . .

Todd: We were always competing. One time our church hired a new youth pastor. John managed to get in good with the guy and his wife. Of course, that meant John would get the best leadership positions in our youth group. It really made me jealous.

A "Friend" in Need . . .

Amid all the competition and conflict, there were a few positives to their relationship. Throughout high school, John tipped the scales to the heavy side—so much so that many of the kids made fun of him for being fat. Not Todd. "I guess I didn't make fun of him because that would have been cruel," says Todd. "True, we were envious of each other. But to use his weight to put him down or to get others to side against him would have been too cruel." Although John never told Todd until years later, John really appreciated his chief rival's silence on the weight topic.

Yet such bits and pieces of potential friendship wouldn't have come together if it weren't for a decision they made independent of each other. They both decided to attend the same Christian college. Somehow, although neither one really wanted it this way, they ended up in the same dorm. And on the same floor.

Yet throughout that first year, they avoided each other, developing separate sets of friends. Then during their sophomore year, John suddenly found himself very much alone—and lonely. He turned to Todd.

John: I'd been dating this girl from home for two years. We were pretty serious, at least that's what I thought; but this one night we were talking on the telephone, and she told me it was over. She wanted to break up. I was crushed. Heartbroken. I had nobody to turn to, so I turned to Todd. While we were far from being good friends, he at least knew the girl. I felt he'd understand the situation.

Todd: It was late when John came to my door. When I saw him, I almost said, "What the heck are you doing here at 2:00 in the morning!" Before I actually said that, though, I looked at his face. I could tell something was wrong. He didn't do anything for the first few seconds. He just stood there with this grim look. After a while, he started crying.

John: I was feeling very rejected. When I finally managed to hold back the tears, I remember asking Todd, "Does anyone really love me? Does anyone really care?" Todd's first response was to give me a big hug. Then he said he loved me and cared for me. Todd was the first guy who ever said anything like that to me. It didn't seem at all weird or strange. In fact, it seemed very macho, very manly in the truest sense of the word.

His demonstration of acceptance had a profound impact on me that night. It let me know that I was somebody. It seemed like all these stupid facades of competition and "I'm better than you, you're better than me" came crashing down that night. I told Todd everything. He sat there and listened. He didn't offer advice; he just listened.

Listening First; Speaking Last

Now in their senior year, Todd and John both agree that their friendship—real friendship—began that night. And it's a friendship that's been nurtured over dozens of cheap burritos at Taco Bell, by a lot of late night campus walks, and during some long, vacation-time drives back to Kansas.

John: When we first became friends it was important that Todd be there to listen, and not throw out a lot of advice. If he'd done that, I would have really been turned off. But because I've learned to trust him, I feel free enough to say, "What do you think I should do?" And that's when he pipes in with advice. When he has a problem, he expects me to do the same. But it has taken a while to get to that point.

Todd: I agree. I remember one situation during our freshman year. I had this problem, and I was just kind of talking about it to anybody who'd listen. John happened to be in the room at the time. Afterward he said, "If anytime you want to talk, that's fine." I remember walking down to my room, thinking, *You're the last person I would talk to*. If he had given me advice right then, I would have been completely grossed out. He had to gain my trust before he could begin offering advice.

The Campus Life Guide

Even today, we both listen to each other a lot more than we give advice. John always hears me out. He doesn't jump all over me, even when he feels he's right. And if it's pretty obvious that what I'm saying is wrong, he still hears me out.

Quirks and Differences

Obviously, some problems are not easily solved through advice-giving, or even through listening. Some problems, both Todd and John say, are created by personality differences.

Take Todd's tendency to push practical jokes beyond John's threshold of tolerance. Like hiding John's mattress in a closet or shooting bottle rockets at him while he's in the shower. There's also Todd's tendency to procrastinate.

Then there was the time Todd and John were driving back to Kansas together in a blinding snowstorm. "Here I was, driving along, trying to keep the car on the road," says John. "My nerves were shot. And Todd started talking in pig Latin. I would ask him a question or try to talk to him, and he would only speak in pig Latin! He did this for an entire hour. I'm thinking, *This guy is nuts!*"

On the other hand, John tends to be too serious at times, too intense. But when he's not in the serious mode, he may do something irritating, like snitch one too many of Todd's personal stash of Oreos. There's also John's "this girl's the one for me" cycle. Says Todd: "John will come to me when he's dating someone and say, 'I went out with this girl last night, and I had the best time I've ever had. It was fun. She has a great walk with the Lord. I just know she's the one.' Well, that relationship will end in a couple of weeks, John will start dating another girl, and he'll come to me and say, 'I went out with this girl last night. . . .' I mean, it's the same thing—over and over, again and again. He doesn't seem to learn."

They choose not to make a big deal out of each other's personality quirks. In fact, some of those differences actually have their good points.

Todd: Call it a contradiction, but even though I'm really bugged at times by John's hyperseriousness, I also admire that part of him. He often brings my devil-may-care attitude back to reality. And I think that intense, serious side of John is what often drives him to achieve a goal.

Once a group of us guys went cliff climbing and our lead man made it up this major cliff. Then he said, "Anyone who wants to can come on up." No way was I going to climb up there! Almost everybody else felt the same way, except John. Now it took him forever to make it to the top, but he made it. Even when things are hard for him, he'll try them anyway. I admire that.

John: While his fooling around ticks me off sometimes, I still appreciate Todd's fun-loving attitude. He can be serious, but then he has a playful spirit. He helps me to loosen up a lot. Here's something else I really admire in Todd: While I tend to stick with the status quo, he isn't afraid to buck the system. Like when the guys in our dorm have a conversation about our Christian beliefs, Todd will ask, "Well, why do you believe that way?" One thing I've learned from him is to think through the reasons I believe as I do. He really challenges me to be real about my faith.

No doubt about it. He's definitely the best friend I've ever had.

"You know what I like about our friendship, Marj? We stick together no matter what."

CHAPTER 16. *Debbi and Kim*

Growing with the Changes

Debbi and Kim's friendship was bound to happen. They shared a locker when Kim first started attending Debbi's high school in Colorado Springs, Colorado. They were also members of the same church youth group and later decided on the same midwestern college, where they've been roommates since day one as freshmen. Debbi and Kim have been best friends for five years. But they both admit their friendship is different now than it was in high school.

Debbi: We haven't grown apart since then; we've just grown differently. I think we're more independent of each other. Kim and I spent ALL of our time together in high school. Now we're still as close, but we're involved in different activities so we don't see each other as much.

Kim: We ran with the same group of friends in high school. Now Debbi and I have branched out—we've found our own interests and friends. But branching out has brought us closer. We don't spend the same amount of time together as we used to, but it's taught us to communicate better.

Debbi: The best thing is just knowing that we care about each other, and that we don't have to worry about "Is she mad at me?" or "What will she think if I do this?" There is complete confidence between us that we'll always be friends.

Differences and Similarities

On the surface, Kim and Debbi are different. Debbi, a computer science and math major, has brown hair, with soft brown eyes to match. Her love for volleyball runs deep. Kim, whose greatest interests include tennis and journalism, has blond hair and friendly blue eyes.

Of her own personality, Debbi says, "I'm more independent and more aggressive than Kim." Kim agrees, explaining, "When Debbi sets a goal, she doesn't just meet it; she goes way beyond it. I tend to just work to meet the goal." But Debbi is quick to talk about Kim's strengths, too: "Both of us are people persons, but she has a real gift for being able to go up to anybody and start a conversation. She's more outgoing than I am." While they are both good students, A's come more naturally for Debbi.

Despite the outward differences, though, it is the similarities that have made them best friends.

Debbi: We enjoy so many of the same things. Both of us appreciate the little things—we get excited about going on a walk, for example. But my favorite part of our friendship is how we can take any situation and make it fun without getting upset over what happens. Like when we got lost in Chicago our freshman year. It wasn't a big deal; we just laughed and had fun with it. And when we end up cross-country skiing for a couple of miles straight uphill, we laugh about it. We have a way of making the bad situations fun. Or we at least look at them in a positive way.

Kim: Fun is a big part of our friendship—everything Debbi and I do is an adventure. Her determination, and the fact that she has no fear whatsoever, rub off on me. When we're skiing, for example, she always encourages me to take risks—to try things I wouldn't try if she weren't with me. My life would be boring without Debbi, although when we're together, I'm never sure if I'm going to live!

Debbi: We have a balance, though, between fun and seriousness. One of the biggest things we share is the understanding that God is at the center of our lives. And out of that comes a lot of encouragement. I also think account-ability is part of it. We don't always sit around and ask, "How's it going with your devotions?" but we can usually tell just because we know each other so well.

Kim: Debbi is more of an encouragement to me than anyone else. I'm pretty confident, but I'm afraid of failure sometimes. She tells me I can do it, and urges me to just go for my goals. But being able to share spiritual things is one of the most encouraging parts of our friendship. I remember that when my grandma had a stroke and died at the end of last semester, Debbi asked if we could pray together. We did, and we were both crying because my grandmother was like a grandmother to her, too. That meant a lot to me.

Through Tough Situations

The past year has been difficult for both of them. Beyond the stress of their studies, activities, and social lives, they each were spending their spare time helping two separate friends through personal crises. Then, when Kim's grand-mother died, it put an additional strain on her.

Kim: With all that had happened in just a few months, I was depressed. When I got home after finals week, I withdrew from my friends. It wasn't anything intentional, but I just felt drawn to my family. I couldn't figure out why I was so sad and why I wanted to be alone so much, but then I thought, *Of course you're depressed—you're dealing with a loss.* I wasn't trying to blow everybody off; I just needed to be alone.

Debbi: Kim's avoidance of me wasn't something I liked, but I tried to be understanding about it. One thing I've learned in my friendships is that a lot of times, when people are really struggling, they withdraw; and I need to leave them alone for a while. It is hard when your friend pulls away, but I knew that's what she had to do. She wrote me a letter during break to explain what she'd been feeling and why. Since she didn't really need me to be there with her in person, I made sure I spent extra time praying for her.

The Campus Life Guide

When There's Just Not Enough Time

Debbi and Kim have had to work through one particular obstacle to their friendship. It's an obstacle that affects most close friendships at some point: a lack of time together.

Kim: I don't see Debbi as much because I'm dating someone seriously now, and because we're both so involved in school. We are trying hard to make time for each other, but I feel guilty about being so busy.

Debbi: It's tough not seeing as much of Kim. I'm not concerned that we'll stop being friends—our friendship is too strong for that. It's just that when you're close to someone, you naturally want to spend time with her. And with Kim dating Jeff seriously, I've had to "share" her—it's no longer automatic that she'll do something with me. It used to be that whatever came up, we'd do it together. Now it's different. Yet she's been sensitive to this, and I try not to make a big deal about it. I see it as my concern—something I need to work out on my own—rather than as a problem between us that we need to talk through.

Kim: I make the effort to give Debbi my time. I'll ask her to meet me for lunch; I send her cards and notes of encouragement; I let her know I'm praying for her. Sometimes I just say, "Hey, let's get away Friday night for dinner and a movie."

Debbi: Those things help. It's nice to know it matters to her that we don't spend as much time together, because I questioned for a while whether it did matter to her. The changes are all a part of growing up, I guess. They're going to happen because it's that time in our lives. Everything is in transition for both of us.

Spending time together is important . . . well, I should say, spending quality time is important. You don't have to be around a person 24 hours a day to be best friends; but when you are with that person, you have to make the most of it.

17. *Drew and Mim*

When a Guy and a Girl Become Best Friends

As members on the cross-country and track teams at college, Drew and Mim's friendship progressed from knowing each other by name, to joking around at meets, to ice fights in the cafeteria, and finally, to more serious talks.

Drew: I see a lot of surface level, guy-girl friendships built around fun, and I see a lot of them that have some depth; but I see very few that have both the fun and the depth. I can talk to Mim about things I rarely share with my other friends. I had a big decision to make last year about whether to get involved in a particular campus organization, and Mim is one of the few people I really talked to about it. And when I was dealing with the breakup of a difficult dating relationship several months ago, she gave me a listening ear, as well as perspective on both sides of the problem.

Mim: Our friendship is very supportive. These past two years of college have been especially difficult for me, but Drew has been there the whole time. He is a great listener and support when it comes to helping me deal with my problems. A few months ago I was struggling with some frustrations that I'd kept bottled up for a long time. Drew was the first one I went to. When I told him my frustrations, he didn't say, "Oh, that's terrible! I can't believe you'd actually feel that way!" He was just very understanding.

Since he's an easygoing person, he helps me get perspective on my emotions and think in a healthier way. Drew also knows the right time to give me a hug or just reach over and squeeze my hand. He knows me so well that I feel I can come to him with anything and not worry about being rejected.

Facing the Inevitable Question

Being able to talk openly is what helped them work through the inevitable question: Should we date? It wasn't a question they could deal with lightly. They both knew how negatively romance could affect a good friendship.

Drew and Angie, for example, had been close friends, and they eventually started dating. When they broke up, their friendship suffered. Mim was very close to Jason until he became romantically interested in her. When she told him it wouldn't work, their friendship changed drastically. So when the question of dating came up for them, Drew and Mim were determined not to make the same mistake with each other.

One Friday evening, in early spring of their junior year, Mim and Drew decided it was time for them to confront that question.

Drew: Coming to a point where we could discuss whether or not to date was a natural progression. We had been spending a lot of quality time together—even if it was just a matter of me walking Mim home and then staying to talk with her until 1:00 A.M. Neither one of us was trying to push our relationship in a romantic direction—although I do think that in any guy-girl friendship there is always the element of "What if . . . ?" We both just started wondering, Are we headed in that direction? It seemed like we were, so we needed to talk it out.

Mim: We had gone to the student union to hear a band play, and then walked back to Drew's apartment. It had been a fun, relaxing evening already, so I felt comfortable when he brought up the subject. We both agreed that you never know what God might have planned for the future, but for now, our friendship alone is too valuable. That's why we decided not to date each other.

Drew: Mim and I knew the risks involved if we ever chose to date each other. We recognized that we were pretty serious about this friendship, and that it was a special thing. We cared about it enough to talk through our feelings because so much was at stake. I think for Mim it was especially encouraging that I even brought up the topic. The year before, I wouldn't have talked about it at all.

Mim: The fact that Drew would initiate such a talk was a small sign to me of where our relationship was going—that it was growing deeper.

The Pluses of Give and Take

Drew says he's learned more about communicating from Mim than from anyone else. And because of Drew, Mim has seen how important it is to make friendship the basis for any relationship.

Drew: One thing that initially impressed me about Mim was her personality. She is a very high-strung, high-energy person with a unique way of relating to others. I tend to be a fairly reserved person, and I don't always express myself very well; but she's one of the few people who can draw me out. By expressing herself as she does, she helps me communicate better.

Mim has influenced me to be a better listener, too. I've been very busy in the pre-med program over the past three years, and with that busyness comes a lot of fatigue. Given the fact that I'm not prone to communicate anyway, it's that much harder for me when I'm tired. But she has taught me that communication doesn't just happen. You have to make it happen.

Mim: One of the greatest things for me is that I've been shown, beyond a doubt, that friendship is the best way to build a lasting relationship. Looking into the future, I think that I would've settled for less of a friendship foundation with the person I marry if I hadn't had Drew as a friend. I've realized that what a romantic relationship adds to a friendship is small in comparison to what a deep friendship already has.

Because we care about each other, and because our ideas on what life is all about are the same, we can really support each other. And those things are going to get me through the painful times a lot more than someone's kisses and touches.

Drew: I can see now how the dividends of what I've learned from Mim are paying off in other relationships. I know that the person I end up marrying, and even the girl I'm dating right now, have a lot to be thankful for because of the friendship Mim and I have had.

Needed: The Right Personalities

Drew and Mim recognize the value in their friendship, but they also realize that not every guy and girl can have the same kind of relationship. A lot of it depends on the personalities involved.

Drew: I think it takes a certain combination of people to relate like Mim and I do. I have no problem putting her on my shoulders, rough housing with her, giving her a hug. It's comfortable for us to do those things, but it wouldn't be comfortable for a lot of people in friendships similar to ours.

Mim: You don't see many solid guy-girl friendships around. They're not easy to attain. Our friendship is something that has grown with time, and I do think it takes a certain blend of personalities. There is just such an understanding between us, and that's why Drew is my best friend.

It was becoming increasingly apparent to Lloyd that the other guys were trying to edge him out of the group.

PART SEVEN

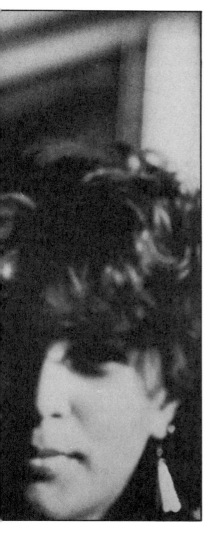

HOW (NOT) TO KILL A FRIENDSHIP

18. *The Destructive Power of Negative Talk*

Who doesn't love a good put-down? We think they're funny. Rodney Dangerfield built his comic career on relating how other people put him down and then lamenting, "I don't get no respect." Put-downs are the foundation of most television sit-coms. There's even a phone line, "Dial an Insult."

Put-downs are also a big part of our everyday communication. You crack a joke at someone else's expense. Your friends laugh and say, "Good line." You feel great. Maybe the other person laughs too, on the outside, but you rarely stop to think how that person might be feeling on the inside.

The Underside of Insults

"Hey, Pizza Face, who hit you with the ugly stick?"

The whole group of guys laughed. There was no one in the hall but them and me. I pretended I didn't hear as I walked quickly to my class, but I felt my face get hot. When I got home that day, I cried. Their words confirmed my worst fear: No guy would ever want to date a girl with acne and glasses.

If it's cool to insult others, it's necessary to stay cool when insulted. You might even laugh along with the others. But you don't forget the remark. You think about it for days.

The person who insults you forgets it easily enough. Confront him with what he said about you, and he may not even believe you. But you know. You carry it around with you like a secret wound.

Why does it hurt? Because words filter down to our subconscious minds. And the subconscious mind does not have a sense of humor. We believe, at the subconscious level, what other people say about us.

The baseball coach told Barry, "You'll make a lousy baseball player." Guess what happened? "I convinced myself that he was right. I just gave up and dropped out of baseball," says Barry. We tend to live down to the names other people call us.

What Are My Friends Hearing?

It's like we all have a cassette player in our brain, and we're recording all those comments—about our shoes, athletic ability, appearance, weaknesses. We play back the tapes to ourselves all the time.

Some comments are carried around for the rest of our lives—hurtful things that somebody tossed out without thinking.

The people in your circle of friends are playing back similar tapes in their brains—recordings of the things you've said that hurt them, things that got back to them somehow. Here's a question to ask yourself: How do your friends feel about themselves after they've been around you? Do they feel bigger, or smaller? Do they feel like more of a person, or do they feel like less of a person?

How to Mug People with Your Mouth

If you really want to hurt people, there are three ways to do it:

Call them names. We never forget the names we've been called. Sometimes we even become the names we're called. (That's what happened when Barry's coach put him down.) Call someone "dumb" enough times, and he'll stop raising his hand in class for fear of saying something stupid.

One way we call people names is by putting them into

categories: jock, cheerleader, burnout, brain, dork, etc. Once we've plunked others into categorized slots, once we've neatly labeled them, we treat them according to the label. As we've already seen, people have a way of conforming to the names they are called.

"Whatever you do, no off-the-wall remarks."

A better approach would be to get to know the person first, before you label him. You might find that the "brain" has a wonderful sense of humor. Or that the "burnout" is really very caring.

Jackie was not quite up to the academic speed of most kids, though she went to regular classes in a regular school. She started coming to her school's Campus Life club meetings. After being in the group for a year, she said, "This is the first place I've ever been in my life where I wasn't called 'retard.'" Every other place, she had not been Jackie, she had been "retard." The Christians in her group, however, accepted her for who she is. And she began to see herself as more than "a retard."

Attack weaknesses. The second way you can hurt a friend with your mouth is to become a shark. When sharks discover there's blood in the water, they get excited. At just the hint of weakness, the sharks close in.

Every school has its share of sharks. You miss that basket that would have won the game. Afterwards, in the locker room, a shark comes up to you, and in front of all your friends says, "You missed, you jerk!" As if you didn't know you messed up.

Wear the wrong thing, say the wrong thing, do the wrong thing, and you get slashed by the sharks.

"The tongue has the power of life and death, and those who love it will eat its fruit" (Proverbs 18:21). Your tongue is the most powerful part of your body. When you use it to attack weaknesses, you're wielding a death-dealing blow. But by holding your tongue, you can not only stop the bleeding—you can also start the healing.

Dump garbage. Sometimes we're like big garbage trucks that back up and unload a heap of trash on top of someone. So often it's our closest friends who get dumped on.

Your best friend borrowed your cassettes again and forgot to bring them back. And now one of your favorites is mangled. You're angry. You call her up and light into her. You inform her she's careless and inconsiderate. While

The Campus Life Guide

you're at it, you tell her that she's obviously too stupid to remember anything, since she can't remember to bring your cassettes back. All warmed up now, you go on to criticize her for her weight, her shyness, and any other weaknesses you can think of. That's dumping.

Or maybe you're just in a bad mood. Anyone who gets in your way is criticized, grumbled at, ignored, or cut down. A truckload of negativity gets dumped on anyone unfortunate enough to cross your path.

When we unload our mess on someone, we may feel better, but the other person is buried under all the stinking trash we've left behind.

"Reckless words pierce like a sword, but the tongue of the wise brings healing" (Proverbs 12:18). A reckless tongue can do a lot of damage. But a wise tongue can actually help put people back together again.

King David prayed, "Set a guard, O Lord, over my mouth; keep watch over the door of my lips" (Psalm 141:3). Imagine a guard over your mouth that doesn't let out anything negative at all.

Making God Cry

You really have an awesome power: You have the power to make God himself cry. Ephesians 4:30 says, "Do not grieve the Holy Spirit." You can actually make God the Holy Spirit grieve the way you grieve and cry over someone who dies. How can you make God weep? By engaging in "bitterness, rage and anger, brawling and slander, . . . every form of malice (verse 31).

God is trying to build up this person you are cutting down. He's trying to let this person know how loved he or she is, how unique and special. Tear down what God's trying to build, and you can see why God would cry. It's like you spent all day building a model airplane—and someone comes over and smashes it. "Oh, I was only fooling around, I'm sorry," the person says casually; but you, like the model airplane, are crushed.

A New Kind of Cool for You and Your Friends

It may be cool in your school to be cruel, but there's a better kind of cool. And you and your friends can start it.

Admit to the negatives of negative talk. If you're tired of tearing down, say it. Admit that you're ready to resign from the demolition crew and apply for the construction crew. That you want to learn how to become a builder-upper of people.

Remember the power of positive talk. Think of a time when your words built someone up. Maybe you noticed that your friend, who is kind of a loner, seemed a little down. And you went up to her and said sincerely, "You look really nice today. You have the nicest clothes, and you always look so put together." Didn't you feel great when she looked at you and smiled, even though she did seem a little embarrassed by your compliment?

Building other people up brings a special bonus: You build yourself up in the process.

Here's a verse worth memorizing: "Do not let any unwholesome talk come out of your mouth, but only what is helpful for building others up according to their needs, that it may benefit those who listen" (Ephesians 4:29). If you want to be on the construction crew instead of the demolition crew, adopt a policy of saying only positive things.

Try positive name-calling. Look for characteristics you can praise in people. We're naturally good at finding the chink in people's armor. It takes extra character to find things to praise. Here's a list to start your search: thoughtful, good sense of humor, generous, helpful, good listener, smart, good-looking, cheerful, fun. Use your own way with words to think up creative, positive names to call people.

Say thank you. When was the last time you thanked a friend for being there? For showing up on time? For helping you with your homework? Show you care by saying it.

Defend the attacked. What's the opposite of a shark? A football player. What? Yes, a football player. When a guy's running down the field with the ball, several people are blocking for him, saying to potential tacklers, "You've got to get me first if you want him." In our relationships, we are meant to be each other's blockers—people who are big enough and strong enough to say, "You'll have to get past me before you can attack the name and reputation of someone I know."

For example, when a shark closes in and says to one of your friends, "Way to go, losing that game for us," you can step up to him and say, "What's your problem? He played a good game." Or when you hear someone spreading a rumor about a person you know, you confront the individual spreading the rumor: "I'm sure that isn't true. I happen to know she would never do a thing like that."

You have tremendous power in that tongue of yours—power to build your friends up or to tear them down. The choice is yours.

—Diane Eble and Ron Hutchcraft

CHAPTER 19.

Those Jealous Feelings

En-vy. 1. A feeling of discontent and resentment aroused by another's desirable possessions or qualities, accompanied by a strong desire to have them for oneself.

Recently, I joined fifteen people from different parts of the country for a week-long tour of four countries in Europe. I enjoyed the sights, the food, and the people, but all week I struggled with something that is both a feeling and a temptation.

What I struggled with was jealousy.

Maybe it was because I didn't really know anyone else that I focused on the externals. It started with the clothes. I didn't have enough of the right things to wear. It spread from envying clothes to being jealous of someone else's looks. I saw how freely many of the other people spent money, and I felt poor. I found myself envying this person's clothes, that person's poise, another person's background. The more I envied others, the worse I felt about myself.

So I've been thinking a lot about envy. About what it does to us, if we let it. (It almost ruined my first-ever trip to Europe.) About what it does to friendships. I've also been talking to people, asking for their thoughts.

What Makes You Jealous?

Todd: I tend to envy qualities that I don't have, like musical ability or high intelligence—things that you either have or don't have. It's not like you can work hard and become more intelligent.

Jealousy raged among Mike's friends as he gloated over his new position as captain of the croquet team.

Michelle: Though I am a musician myself, I'm still jealous of others who are more musically talented than I. There's a fine line between healthy competition and jealousy. When I was trying out for college scholarships, I felt very competitive against others.

Conney: I envy people who get good grades, like my best friend. I also get jealous of girls who are prettier than I.

April: If your friend gets a new car for her birthday, and you know your parents will never buy you a car, you can't help but feel jealous.

Todd: Your social status is based on things like clothes and cars and money. The attitude lots of people have is,

"You can't eat with us, go to the game with us, go to our parties"—and you know it's based on stuff like what kind of car you drive, what clothes you wear ,and what your parents do for a living. So I find myself envying others for what they have.

Rebecca: I think everyone is jealous of the kind of people who don't have to work at anything, yet who just keep succeeding. But I'm also jealous of people who are popular. And it's the worst when I'm jealous of someone because a guy I like is interested in her, not me.

April: I'm jealous of my friends who have parents who let them do things my parents don't let me do. My parents are a lot stricter than lots of my friends' parents.

Jim: They'd never know it, but I'm jealous of my friends who come from whole families. My parents are divorced.

How Envy Affects Us

Envy does three things:

It blinds us. When we focus on what we don't have, it's nearly impossible to see what we do have.

It enslaves us. As I focus on what you have that I want, the feeling that I should have it becomes a deeper, burning desire: "I must have it." If I don't have it, something tells me I'm not good enough. I'm lacking something essential.

It hurts our friendships. Sometimes it means friendships never happen. Often it means friendships are torn apart.

The Bible says it plainly: "What causes quarrels and fights among you? Don't they come from your desires that battle within you? You want something but don't get it. You kill and covet, but you cannot have what you want . . ." (James 4:1–2).

Jealousy Hurts Friendships

Rebecca: Jealousy ruined my relationship with my best friend. We had a perfect friendship, for a while. But she and I had a different set of friends, and that came between us. Her friends were more into drinking, smoking, and sex. My

The Campus Life Guide

friends didn't do those things, and we got better grades and were more respected. I think she was jealous of me and my friends. I didn't like her friends and didn't like seeing her get swallowed up by them. We finally talked it out, and at least now we can speak to each other, but we're not close anymore.

Jeffery: My best friend and I fell into a spirit of competition that sometimes went too far. If I had something, he had to have it, and vice versa. We'd try to outdress each other, outdo each other—in everything from grades to who we hung around with.

Michelle: Jealousy ruined a friendship for me. My best friend and I both tried out for a play. She was a senior; I was a sophomore, and I got the lead part. (She didn't get any part.) My friend was so jealous, she actually hurt me physically. For instance, I asked her to help me with a costume, and she stuck me with a pin. Another time she hit me with a hammer when we were working on a set. She made everything look like an accident. I didn't say anything to anyone; I tried to "kill her with kindness." But we haven't spoken to each other since the play.

The Importance of Realizing You're Jealous

To keep jealousy from ruining our friendships, we have to admit to ourselves that the feeling is there. This isn't always easy. We may feel guilty for being jealous of our best friend. We may feel unspiritual for wanting nice clothes so badly. But admitting the truth about our feelings is the first step to dealing with them.

During my Europe trip I had to wrestle with my values. I had to remind myself that who I am is more important than what I have (or don't have). I had to refuse to be intimidated by what these other people had, and try to build relationships anyway.

It was hard to do. I'm not sure I could have done it without a spiritual orientation: reminding myself of what the Bible says, and praying through my feelings and values.

Faith Battles Envy

Conney: Before I became a Christian, there were lots of people I would have liked to change places with. But now that I am a Christian, I'm realizing that God has made things a certain way for a reason. I may not know the reason now, but someday I will. I can feel better about what I have and don't have.

Jim: I tend to bury my feelings when I'm jealous. Sometimes the feelings go away; sometimes they come up in another way. But lots of times I'll write out my feelings, then tear up the paper later. And it helps when I pray about it.

April: I remind myself that if God wants me to have something, he'll give it to me.

Jeffery: I have to constantly remind myself that my identity is in Christ, not in what I have.

Rebecca: Last year my best friend and I liked the same guy. I really had a hard time with jealousy. But one day I found the verse in 2 Corinthians 6:14 about not being yoked with unbelievers. God used that verse to show me that this guy wasn't right for me anyway. It changed my perspective.

Todd: I've found prayer really helps a lot. I pray that God would help me work out my feelings. I remember Philippians 4:11-13, about being able to do all things through Christ. I pray for a happy, grateful heart.

The Pros and Cons of Saying, "I'm Jealous of You"

When we're jealous of others, should we confront them about it? That may or may not be helpful, depending on how close you are to the person. Sometimes it's better to work through the feelings yourself. Sometimes it helps to talk to someone, even if it's not the person you're jealous of. But in a close relationship, it's probably a good idea to talk about how you feel.

Rebecca: I usually try to work out my feelings first by

myself. I pray a lot about it, talk through my feelings with myself. But if I can't work through them on my own, I'll talk with the person I'm jealous of. I'll let my friend know how I feel.

Jeffery: My best friend and I eventually realized how unnecessary all our competition was, and we moved beyond it. We'd talk about it indirectly in our Bible study group— like we were talking about other people; but we were really talking about what jealousy was doing to us, and we both knew it. Now we're better friends, and we aren't as competitive or jealous.

Michelle: My roommate at college is very pretty. At first I was real jealous of her. She is kind of reserved, so I initially thought she was acting superior. But one day she asked my advice about a problem she was having with her boyfriend, and that showed me she was willing to be open with me. Eventually I told her I felt jealous of her. She said she has always struggled with shyness, and other people have mistaken her shyness for being stuck-up. We've been the best of friends since our talk. I'm glad I kept an open mind toward her.

Handling a Friend's Jealous Feelings

Should we confront a person we suspect is jealous of us? That also depends on the relationship. We can do something about our own feelings of jealousy, but we can't change another person. All we can do is try to work it out.

Todd: Last summer I got a part in a church skit and my best friend didn't. I invited him to spend the night after I got the part, and we talked. He admitted he felt hurt. I said I understood how he felt, and we prayed that this would draw us together and not rip our friendship apart. Now when we see jealousy creeping in, we talk about it. We'll admit it's happening again, and we'll pray about it.

Michelle: When my friend was so jealous of me for getting the part in the play, I talked about the situation with a close friend from school, and also with my pastor. They thought I should talk to her, but I was more comfortable just letting the friendship die.

Jim: If I sense someone's putting me off, I'll try to talk to the person one-on-one. If he's jealous, I try to point out what he has going for him that he's not even aware of.

What I Did About My Own Jealous Feelings

I did work through my envious feelings during my week in Europe. I reached out to people, in spite of my feelings of insecurity. And I discovered something: Underneath all the apparent success and sophistication and nice clothes, many of these people were both hurting and searching. The "rich kids" weren't really so rich where it counted. The person whose looks I envied talked about how confused she was about relationships, how scared she was of marriage because of her parents' divorce. The guy who obviously had lots of money confessed how it hurt to have people use him for his money. He told me wistfully, "You seem like such a happy person."

At that moment, I realized how much I really do possess. And the last of my envy gave way to something else: gratitude.   —Diane Eble

"Very nice, Bruno, and you worked that all by yourself?"

to Making and Keeping Friends 139

CHAPTER 20. *Other Friendship Killers*

These things kill friendship. Dead. If you want to make and keep friends, avoid them.

Deceitfulness. Call it lying, disloyalty, or being two-faced. In a poll of Campus Life readers, this killer came out as the worst. Said one student: "What bothers me most about a friend is when he talks about me behind my back; when he's dishonest, two-faced." Turn against a friend—and expect them to turn and walk away from you. But be honest, up front, loyal—and expect friendship to happen.

Gossip. Teeter-totter principle: I bring myself up by tearing you down. "Do you know what I see/saw?"

Selfishness. Self-centered friends. They're in the middle, nudging everybody to the outermost edge so they can make more space for themselves. There's room in the middle for everyone. Make space; you'll have more friends.

Competition. Friendship is not a race we run as competitors. Instead, we should cheer each other on.

Negativism. True, misery loves miserable company. Up to a point. Beyond that, your complaining will make friends scarce.

Greed. If things come before friends, pretty soon all you'll have are things.

Snubbing. You're here; you're not here. I only see you when I want to. A student expressed it this way: "It's so annoying when your friend leaves you out. Maybe she'll start

The Campus Life Guide

a conversation with a new person and she'll forget you're even there. You try to talk, but she just forgets you're there."

Pushiness. Call it hyper-peer pressure. It comes down to this: "You do this and I'll be your friend." If you want friends, you'll respect them for who they are and for what they believe in.

Critical attitude. You become my judge and jury. You decide the verdict on my every action—and I'm always guilty. Won't you take the time to look for the positive me?

Closed. Hello? Anybody in there? Won't you please talk to me? Friends communicate best by communicating.

No time. I'm busy; you're busy. But if this friendship is important, we have time for each other.

Users unfriendly. Friends who use friends to get something only want something—they don't want a friend.

Promise-breaking. I'll do it . . . I really will. But I forget, all the time. Keep a promise; keep a friend.

—Jim Long

CHAPTER 21.

Forgiving When a Friend Hurts You

Kris: Karyn and I were best friends in high school. She was taller than I, with a dark complexion and brown eyes that the guys really fell for. We shared a love of running, so we were on the same track team. But our friendship really began my sophomore year (her freshman year), during a youth group fund-raiser.

Karyn played a piano solo for that evening's talent show, one of the few "talent" portions of the whole night. I was about to go on stage for my comedic performance when I saw her just coming off stage. I spontaneously gave Karyn a quick hug and said, "You sounded great." Then I was off to do my routine.

Later that evening, during the get-together following the program, Karyn came and sat beside me. We'd known each other by name for a long time, but had never really been involved because we'd gone to different schools. That evening was our beginning point.

Karyn was dealing with some difficult things at home— her parents were divorced—and the conversation between us turned to those problems. We ended up talking for more than an hour, and I walked away from the evening impressed with her warmth and honesty.

We spent a lot of time together at church during that year; so when she started attending my high school in tenth grade, we quickly became inseparable. We both ran cross-country and track, and the two of us put in many weekend evenings at the mall, just talking.

Don't get me wrong—it wasn't an exclusive friendship. Karyn and I had many friends, and we each were seeing a guy. But we called each other "my best friend." We could talk about everything, and we did. Our friendship was unique, I think, for both of us.

When I became a senior, our talks focused a lot on "what happens next year." We were both concerned that my being in college and her in high school would affect our friendship. Everyone said, "Just wait. You'll lose touch and things will change between you." We told the doubters (and ourselves), "No, we're different than the people who let that happen." As it turns out, the doubters were right.

The Problems Begin

I first suspected there was trouble when Karyn's long-distance letters became more newsy and superficial. She told me less and less about her feelings and more about who was dating whom at school. When I'd call her, she was distant. But I didn't want to assume there was a problem. Sometimes it's hard to really talk when you're one thousand miles and three states apart.

We spent time together during my winter break, but after that . . . nothing. Not a letter. Not a card. Not a phone call. I worried about the silence. Had I done something to make her angry? Were we drifting apart, as everyone had said we would, or was Karyn just busy?

During spring break of my freshman year, I called Karyn from Florida (where my two roommates and I were spending the week with my parents). We just talked news for a few minutes, then I said, "Karyn, I haven't heard from you since Christmas, and I'm not sure why. Is something wrong?"

Her answer shocked me: "My feelings have changed. We can still be friends if you want, but we can't be best friends." She went on to say that she'd realized, during my absence, that she had missed spending time with some of her other good friends.

I don't even remember the rest of our conversation; I only remember how much I hurt.

Facing My Emotions

I was deeply hurt, but I was also angry. How could a three-year best friendship change in only a few months' time?

And her remark about missing time with her other friends really cut me. Many times Karyn had insisted on doing something with me rather than somebody else, saying, "You're graduating first. These people will be here after you're gone—so I want to spend time with you while I can." I didn't feel she should accuse me when the choice had been hers.

At the same time, I started having problems with another friend—someone both Karyn and I were close to. We worked things out in the next few weeks, but this mutual friend admitted that she and Karyn had said some cruel things about me. When I heard that, I was hurt even more. Best friends aren't supposed to stab each other in the back.

Although I was very hurt and very angry, a dark vein of guilt and blame ran through me. Whenever I reflected on what had happened, I always came back to me. What had I done wrong? How could I have worked harder to keep Karyn's friendship? Karyn had said, "I've changed," but I still felt like what had happened was my fault.

I thought back through the three years we'd spent together and blamed myself for everything I'd done wrong—some of the petty arguments I'd started, the remark I'd made a few Christmases before about her dad, my failure to help her with a science project. I kept thinking, *Well, maybe if I hadn't made those mistakes, she'd still want to be my best friend.* That thought crossed my mind many, many times: *If only I could've been a better friend. . . .*

It took a long time before I even began to confront my feelings about this whole situation.

Steps of Forgiveness

Not every friendship—not even most friendships—change as Karyn's and mine did. But if it happens, the following steps should help you to forgive and to give your friendship a chance to be renewed.

Evaluate the situation. The problem could be something you said or did. If so, you need to make things right.

But it's also possible that your friend was struggling with another problem, unrelated to you. If this is the case, you can be a help by forgiving him or her immediately and trying to find a way to help your friend.

Share your pain with someone who knows you. Usually, problems should remain between you and the person involved. But if you've tried to resolve things with that friend, and you're uncertain about the next step, try talking through your feelings with a person who doesn't know your friend. (Don't use your friend's name either. Anonymity is essential.) The purpose is not to gossip, but to get objective advice from someone who knows you well.

The "third person" I talked to helped me realize that Karyn and I were both responsible for the falling-out of our friendship. I could be angry with Karyn for talking about me to others, and I could be hurt because she didn't want us to be close anymore; but Karyn had a right to be upset with me, too. I hadn't been good at expressing my feelings, and I had expected too much of our friendship. We shared the blame.

Pray about your feelings. I knew I needed to give God all the pain and the guilt and the anger, but I knew healing would take time, too. I'd been rejected by a person I cared very much about. Only God could be my strength as I slowly dealt with all the emotions I experienced.

Write a letter. Several months after the Florida phone call, I wrote Karyn: to apologize for putting such big expectations on our friendship (because by this time I had seen how my insecurities and immaturity had affected it); to acknowledge how good a friend she'd been to me for three years; and to confront Karyn with her broken promises and false accusations. I ended the letter by saying that I hoped we could at least work out the sore spots and be friends.

Although I sent my letter, it's not a good idea for everyone. Letters can be misunderstood, and if you're not around to explain, hurt feelings can become even more painful. I do recommend writing, whether you send the letter or not. Getting the feelings on paper is very helpful.

Forgive and forget. A few weeks after I sent my letter, I got a short response from Karyn. She apologized for hurting me, for breaking her word, but she also reaffirmed her decision—that we could be friends, but not close friends. At that point, I knew I had a choice: I could spend the rest of my life clinging to bitterness, or I could allow God to help me let go of it. Forgiveness is a long process—a lesson that I have to relearn every day. It's not a onetime event.

During three years of prayers and admitting my anger at Karyn before God, he taught me, gradually, that I had to move out of my unforgiving attitude. I couldn't establish other good friendships unless I learned to trust people again and really forgive Karyn.

Reestablish the friendship. Not all friendships will fall apart, as mine and Karyn's did. I have had several relationships where a willingness to forgive brought us back together. But both parties must want the relationship to continue.

Reestablish trust. This doesn't happen immediately; it takes time. If you have betrayed a friend, or if a friend has betrayed you, there will naturally be a time of "testing." For example: If you have lied about a friend, you will need to "prove" that you are worthy of his or her renewed trust. Then, as your friend sees that you are consistently honest, he'll begin to trust you more.

The Campus Life Guide

Some Concluding Thoughts about Karyn

Not too long ago I saw Karyn again. We were both at a bus station, awaiting our transportation. When Karyn noticed me, she rushed up, gave me a hug, and asked how I was doing. And you know, I really was glad to see her. That's when I knew for sure that I had forgiven Karyn. I still cared about her; I didn't recall all the negative things that had happened . . . it was just nice to talk with her again.

On the ride home, I thought about forgiveness. It had come so slowly. Yet it had definitely come. The memory of what had happened between us was still there, but the bitterness and blame had faded. It was a strange feeling.

Some of my high-school friends still mention Karyn occasionally, and it makes me wonder how she's really doing. But most of the time I wonder without anger anymore. God has used the years to bring me to this point— a point of forgiveness. And that is his doing, not mine.

"Your mother and I are beginning to worry, Everett . . . are you letting your friends walk all over you again?"

PART EIGHT

WHEN FRIENDS MOVE AWAY

22. *Losing the Friend I Just Found*

Joan was all I ever wanted in a friend—fun, pretty, loving, fresh, creative, intelligent. We found each other in the crowded confusion of registration line on the first day of camp. There was something special about her that made her stand out from the other two hundred new faces around me—some mysterious chemistry that made me feel she was an old friend from long ago, and we were just picking up where we had left off.

During the week an invisible magnet kept pulling Joan and me together. We went out of our way for each other. She would drop by my cabin on her way to the swimming pool, even though the pool was in the opposite direction. When I ended up at the back of the lunch line, she forfeited her up-front spot just so she could stand and talk with me.

I'd give up horseback riding to go canoeing with Joan. When we sat on logs around the campfire, watched movies in the pavilion, or listened to a speaker in chapel, the seat next to me was always reserved for Joan. She was a warm, secure, happy feeling for me.

I felt safe with Joan—as if I could bring her into my room without having to rearrange the furniture or clean up the mess. She didn't probe the areas that I wasn't yet willing to open for public inspection. Yet, somehow, I felt I could trust her, even with my closed doors and my closets.

Joan and I never had to work at conversation—it just

came. We talked about our pasts and our dreams for the future, but mostly we talked about the present—about guys and dates, about which kind of pop we liked best and why, how stupid we thought the summer fashions were, how the dew rises, where sand dollars come from, and why paddling a canoe works better when you kneel. Sometimes we didn't even talk. Just being together was enough.

When the Good Times End

The last day of camp was like a funeral. I had only known Joan for seven days, and yet, in those seven days we'd shared a lifetime. Now it was Saturday, and everything was about to change. She was heading for Florida. I was moving on later for Pennsylvania. I carried her suitcase to the bus, waved good-bye, and watched the trail of dust disappear down the road. Joan and I never crossed paths again.

The week had ended. A comfortable little puzzle that fit perfectly together had been torn apart, and now I had to pick up the pieces and start all over again. I walked the beach and watched the waves.

I felt the waves inside—restless, changing feelings that tumbled all over each other. Those waves were like my life— always changing, even when I desperately wanted things to stay the same. It was the ebb and the flow that brought the hurt and the emptiness of happy moments gone—the pain of separation.

I don't know why God made tides that ebb and flow, sands that shift, waves that never crash in exactly the same spot. I don't understand why seasons come and go: why the green leaves of summer turn into the bleak, gray branches of winter; why the crimson tulip has to disappear and go underground before it can bloom again; or why the winds swing around and blow from the north.

I don't understand why good friends and good times come and go; why God doesn't give us beautiful moments on a cassette for instant replay whenever we want them. I don't know why, just when you really learn to like someone, he or she moves away; or why, when you finally find a geometry teacher you can understand, they change your section; or why half of the happy, comfortable homeroom crowd from last year gets sent to a new school.

I don't know why things change—why nothing ever stays the same. Camp does end. Fall comes. Friends get on a bus and ride away, leaving empty holes in your life. The tide ebbs and flows. Leaves shrivel and die. Tulips move underground. The earth shifts on its axis and a season is past.

If Friendships Have to End—Why Take the Risk?

What do I do with the season past? Glibly discard it with all the other disposable, throw-away, easy-come/easy-go commodities of our society?

Or forget the past? Pull myself back inside and never again venture into someone else's life? You never hurt if you've never loved. You never miss what you've never known.

Through the kaleidoscope of change I look for meaning, and the meaning I find is this: For every season of my life, God has a purpose. And if God has a reason, then I am free to go ahead and love even though I know camp ends in seven days, or graduation is only nine months away, or my next-door neighbor may move in a year. I will reach out and embrace friendship without fear of the risk that soon it may end, for through this friendship God wants me to learn, to love, to receive, to give. I will allow my roots to cling deeply to the soil around me even though I know that the deeper the roots, the harder it will be to pull them up someday.

And when things begin to change and God turns over the well-worked soil of my experience, I know that a new growing period is about to begin. That's how God works in his world, a world which never stays the same.

—Ruth Senter

23. Long-Distance Relationships

Kris: As Ruth learned from her friendship with Joan, change is hard, but the growth that occurs because of change is good. Knowing that doesn't make it any easier, though. I know.

While I was growing up, my family moved every three or four years. I hated it—packing up the room that I'd called my own, saying good-bye, beginning the first day of school with no friends, eating that first lunch by myself, trying to find my way to class down unfamiliar hallways, facing the stares of people who wondered where this stranger had come from. Everything about starting over was dreadful to me.

Yet in some strange way, moving helped me. I got to meet many new people; I learned to give each place and new face a chance. I had different opportunities in music and sports and my classes at each school; I learned to get involved. I had to overcome my shyness and be more open with strangers; I learned to be more flexible. The changes made me grow, no matter how reluctantly I faced them.

But when my friend Diann moved to California two years ago, I had a different sort of adjustment to make: I was the one left behind. I'd always been the person doing the leaving; now I had to adjust to the fact that someone I really cared for had left me to go 2000 miles away.

Diann and I had spent a lot of time together. We often got

together for Saturday breakfasts. Or she'd fix up a picnic and we'd go to the park for lunch.

Then one day the word came: "I'm moving to California in the middle of June." I wasn't surprised—I knew she would eventually move once school was out. But expecting her to leave "someday" didn't make it hurt less when "someday" became "today."

How to Keep the Friendship Growing

Diann has been in California for two years now, yet we're as close as we ever were. I can think of several things we've done—things you can do in your own long-distance friendships—to keep the relationship growing.

1) Still make time for each other. Diann and I can't see each other weekly any more, but our friendship continues to be a priority to us. We give it the same kind of time we give the other priorities in our lives. I'll send a card just to say, "I've been thinking about you." We regularly write or call. She'll occasionally send a book to me.

2) Hold on to the "rituals" of your friendship. For example, Diann and I both love to read, so whenever we talk on the phone or write, we'll recommend the best of the latest books we've read.

If you're both really into music, you can make tapes of your favorite songs and send them to your friend. Or, if your friend used to come to your games or performances, videotape them and send a copy. Or take pictures and share them with your friend.

3) Share the good and the bad. As different honors have come my way, I've made sure Diann was one of the first to know about them. And when I'm down or trying to figure out what to do, she has sometimes been the only one I've talked to. It's important to talk through your feelings about things. That way your friend feels like he or she is still a part of your life.

4) Talk about the struggles of being apart. Be honest about the doubts or insecurities you have regarding your

faraway friend. I went to California a month ago to see Diann, and it was a great trip. Part of the reason I went was because I felt like we were starting to grow apart, and I didn't want that to happen. I told her my concern, and we ended up talking about what each of us needs the other to do to remain close despite the long distance. Being apart isn't easy; talking out or writing out these concerns helps prevent misunderstandings in your relationship.

5) Be willing to make sacrifices for your friendship. I gave up a week of my time and quite a bit of money to visit her in California. I could've used the money I'd saved toward the digital piano I want to buy, but I felt that going to see Diann was more important. A piano can wait; friendship can't.

6) Trust God to be faithful. He brought you two together as friends, and he'll be faithful to bring along other friends, too. You've got to believe God's promise that he will provide for all your needs. Everyone needs friends. God knows this. He will provide.

7) Be open to new friendships. Others won't be able to replace your friend, but they can help fill the void. Neither Diann nor I shut ourselves off from the people around us when she moved. We worked to maintain our friendship, but we also knew it was important to surround ourselves with other friends who were closer by.

When You Do Lose Touch

Not all my friendships have remained strong. I think of Jackie, one of my best friends in junior high. We lost contact after my freshman year of college. And I think of John, a good buddy of mine in high school. I spent many hours talking with him and planning pranks with him in band. We wrote for a while, but once he started college, the letters stopped.

Life does get in the way sometimes. I've lost touch with many friends, gradually. No hard feelings. It just happened. And I still have the memories and the good things I learned from my past friendships. But there are some people that

The Campus Life Guide

WHEN CHANGE COMES

"In August I called Jenny and she told me she was moving far away. I have many other friends, but I felt very lonely when she was gone. I felt like a big piece of me was missing and that it could never be filled again.

"Jenny and I started writing each other. As a result, we have grown closer and closer together despite the distance between us."

—Amy, Kemp, Texas

"My friend recently moved to a foreign country. We used to talk to each other all the time; now it takes a month to get a letter from her. I never realized how much I would really miss her. I guess I always took that friendship for granted."

—Jennifer, Medford, Oregon

"I met my new friend, Linda, at a youth retreat some time ago. While we live quite a distance from each other, we keep in touch through letters and a phone call once in a while. I've come to really trust her a lot."

—Timothy, Houston, Texas

"Even though Pam is over 800 miles away, and I can't see her, we still feel close spiritually. In our letters, we both express our needs to each other and ask for prayer during crises. I know that Pam prays for me daily, and I do the same for her."

—Bridget, Moore, Oklahoma

stay your friends for a lifetime, regardless of how things change. There are some friendships that don't change, that won't change, no matter how much the circumstances do. Especially if you're both committed to keeping your friendship alive and growing.

"I just can't stand her . . . she only dresses that way to attract more friends."

The Campus Life Guide

PART NINE

THE CHRISTIAN SIDE OF FRIENDSHIP

24. How Different Should a Christian Be?

For me, the desire to fit in, to be liked and to like other people, has always been a big motivation. I have to admit that an awful lot of what I do and say is determined by my concern for what other people will think.

That bothers me, because all my life I've heard people say, "Christians are supposed to be different." I know the Bible is very clear in teaching that Christians should practice standards of thought, speech, and behavior different from the world's. But how does that relate to that very basic part of my nature which longs for acceptance?

I've seen Christians try to answer this question in almost completely opposite ways.

Some seem to believe that true Christians should never try to "fit in." They choose to be glaringly different. Some plaster Christian bumper stickers on their cars and lockers, or carry a Bible on top of their stack of school books. They may even make a point to loudly exchange "Praise the Lord's" when they meet fellow Christians in the halls between classes.

On the other extreme are Christians who don't seem to believe that there need be any visible difference between them and the rest of the world. For them, it's what's inside that matters—an inner difference of the heart. The no-outward-difference Christians seem to feel that the more closely they identify with our culture, the easier it will be for them to attract others to a relevant faith.

That brings us back to the dilemma. How different should I be?

Fitting in and Standing Out

There's the hint of an answer when Jesus said that Christians are supposed to be the salt of the earth. Salt doesn't serve any purpose apart from the food which it preserves or seasons. Neither can I, as a Christian, be an effective influence on others if I separate myself from them or live so differently that they want to steer clear of my strange ways.

And yet, even when salt penetrates a food, it's still salt. It seasons, but it never becomes meat or potatoes or broccoli. So, too, as a Christian I must maintain a distinction, a flavor that is different. I must never become (or act) non-Christian.

Still, knowing when to fit in and where to stand out is often a problem. When my friends in gym class start telling dirty jokes, I don't feel right about laughing just to go along with them and fit in. But neither do I think I ought to interrupt and give a big sermon on the Bible's view of the sanctity of sex. Should I just sit there and not laugh, or should I get up and leave to show my lack of approval?

What happens when the teacher gets called out of the room during a test, and half the class starts sharing answers?

How do I react when a group of friends invites me to go to a movie I've heard is sexually explicit?

What do I do at a party where some people are starting to get wild?

How much do I say when one of the guys on my ball team swears constantly or when someone tries to share the latest gossip?

How can I make my Christian standards clear without

condemning or ruining my relationship with non-Christian friends? In other words, how different should I be?

A Four-point Strategy

I haven't found any easy answers. And the dilemma is complicated by the fact that God doesn't expect every one of us to react the same way to every situation. Your style for taking your stance as a Christian may be quite different from mine.

But if you struggle with this as much as I do, there are a few basic strategies that can help keep our "differentness" in perspective.

1) Knowing what the Bible says God expects from us is absolutely essential. I've seen many people struggle with a decision without ever knowing or checking to see that the Bible has some very clear teaching on their problem. And often, when the Bible doesn't seem to speak directly to a contemporary situation we face, a little study will uncover some general principles that definitely apply.

2) Praying for God's guidance on a regular basis can show us the best response in many situations. I believe this because of my own experience. But I continue to be ashamed at the number of times I forget to ask God for any direction he wants to give me about how or when I should take a stand for him.

3) Jesus himself taught a very basic overall strategy for making sure non-Christians recognize his followers. He said, "They will know you by your love." This standard of love isn't an easy out. It's not simply an inner difference, a warm fuzzy feeling that only our best friends will notice. True love, with its real concern and compassion for other people, presents some definite behavioral requirements.

If I'm taking a position and choosing to be different because of an unselfish concern for other people, I may not be ostracized for it. Those who can be different and still love those they are different from will often maintain their friendships.

to Making and Keeping Friends   167

4) I don't need to feel guilty about wanting to be accepted, to belong, to fit in. I do, however, need to make certain my desire to be accepted by my friends takes a back seat to my desire to be acceptable to God.

It's a constant choice I have to make. And it seldom seems like a life or death matter.

But it is.

Every time I choose to be different in the way God wants me to be, I grow stronger as a person and as a Christian. When I don't, my Christian life begins to blight and die.

—Gregg Lewis

"I hope you can resolve your identity crisis, Dave . . . Harold . . . whoever."

I Liked God; Stu Didn't

Chris: One afternoon in late August I began college at Iowa State University. There I met a blond Easterner named Stu, my roommate. I soon discovered a difference in our likes and dislikes: I liked God; Stu didn't. And he had some unusual ways of showing it.

Take the dresser on the back wall of our room. Mid-dresser, at the top of the mirror, Stu taped a makeshift chart: CHRISTIANS/LIONS. With each verbal punch at God, Stu hash-marked "Lions." A slam at something irreligious (at times I just had to cut loose), and I got my own mark under "Christians."

Yet amid the put-downs, Stu and I became close—like brothers. While he could attempt to fold, spindle, and mutilate my belief, nobody else dared. Over meals I would bow and pray. Some upperclassman in a Farm-All hat would interrupt, "Why thank God? You should thank the farmers who grew the stuff." (Remember, we were in Iowa.) Stu would get hot and cuss at the guy. Smiling, I would quietly begin my meal.

Most days Stu and I walked the half mile to central campus together. We also attended a lot of weekend concerts, and window shopped at the local music stores. While I made Christian friends, none was like Stu. None as crazy. None as close. His zany lampooning taught me to laugh more, and his open personality taught me to be open more.

And he had plenty he could have hidden. He was insecure. His anger would flare up like the propane in chem lab. He had little patience—especially with himself. Needless to say, we helped each other through many down times.

At the end of the year, Stu went back East; I went back to Indiana. I didn't attend ISU the next fall; I went into the Army. We lost contact. I lost my best friend. After two years in olive drab I got out, bought a car, and swung up to Highway 80 West. I drove some five hundred miles, hoping Stu would still be at Iowa State.

When I stepped out of the Wilson dorm elevator, I didn't find Stu in the old room, but he still lived on the floor. There was Stu, with his stringy strands of blond hair several inches longer than my regulation haircut. After a hug and some brief updates on each other's lives, he mentioned a new release by a rock group we had both liked. He told me about some religious song on the album. The two brothers in the group "had gotten converted," he said. He assured me—with that same irreverent wit—that he hadn't. Still the same Stu. The same best friend.

On his way home during Christmas break, he slipped down Highway 80 East and stopped by my house in Indiana. During his visit, we went out to party with some of my Christian friends. The evening ended with some of the people praying. Stu prayed. Nothing special. He just thanked God for our friendship and hoped all the religious people there would keep the faith. Stu wasn't joking. Not yet a believer himself, but concerned about me—and the faith of the others who were my friends. He was thinking. He was changing, slowly.

Somewhere in the rush of finishing my own schooling and just getting on with life, I lost touch with Stu again. But I'll never forget him. He changed me—helped make me a better person. And I believe my influence changed him eternally—I hope. What more could I, could anybody, ask from a friendship?

25. The Difference Gary Made

Certainly, the best way to influence friends with your faith is by example. I know this from experience. No, this isn't a story about me influencing others. It's about my friend Gary, a guy who literally changed my life. Ours is a relationship that I hope will challenge you as you seek to make new friends and influence old ones.

Our relationship had a painful beginning for me. We were players on opposing eighth-grade football teams. You don't easily forget a face that runs by you touchdown after touchdown.

The next year, as a freshman in geometry, I saw that smiling face again (actually it was the back of his head), this time in the seat in front of me. Thus the beginning of the most significant relationship of my short life—which is very nice when you're going through what seems to be the most insignificant class of your life.

I didn't commit my life to Christ that freshman year, nor did the idea occupy much of my thinking as a sophomore or a junior. But I did do some serious thinking about Gary's life-style and mine, both of which I watched closely.

Looking back, the difference was this: My activities generally seemed to drag either myself or others down to all that is crummy in life. Gary represented the only force on the horizon pushing people upward.

Life at home was miserable: I caused my family many

hardships with a cruel attitude, a quick tongue, and a fiery temper. The excitement of brushes with the law was never very satisfying. Some of my relationships with girls were not exactly the best, either.

I Knew There Was a God Because I Knew Gary

I knew there was a God. I occasionally tuned in to religious programs on Sunday mornings. I once won a plastic cross at the ringtoss booth at the local carnival (I was aiming for the pocket knife). Someone handed me a David Wilkerson "Chicken" tract at the beach when I was 12 (one of the greatest hit-and-run jobs I've ever witnessed). I once read a book on mealtime prayers when I was invited to eat dinner with a Catholic friend's family and was afraid I would be asked to say the blessing.

But most of all, I knew there was a God because I knew Gary. No, Gary was not Jesus, but neither was his life as a Christian confined to a cross on a chain or a bumper sticker. The good news of the gospel was a deep experience for him. As we spent time together—on the student council, playing basketball, he helping me with geometry problems— the stark contrast between the godly and the godless became evident.

I remember some words I wrote in an essay for senior English. I called it "Spaces to Fill." It was aimed at somebody, anybody who might fill them:

"OK, I admit it. I am insecure. I am immature. I am a great waste to the world. But will you help me? Will you get me out of this mess? I need you to help me get out of the dark. Will you be the one to shine the light on me?"

God must have been listening. Two months after that essay was written, he brought people—a small, loving, praying group of them—into my life to help me find my way to Jesus Christ.

So began my life as a Christian. It was tremendously exciting and exhilarating. God was indeed real. "Believe in him!" I'd urge my pagan friends Jim and Tony, because I knew he answered prayer. Mom and Dad must have seen the difference in my life too—the Bible was now getting equal time with Hugh Hefner as post-homework reading.

Bliss. What better word could describe those first two weeks?

And what better term to describe the next two years than roller coaster?

Jesus continually taught his followers that the secret to the kingdom of God is to hear the word of the king and act upon it. "Consistent in the hearing and incredibly sporadic in the doing" aptly described my first few years as a Christian.

A remarkable tolerance for sin, an ox's stubbornness, praying for one thing but doing another—these were traits characterizing my Christian life. But, thankfully, Gary responded to God's asking him to be a friend to this struggling Christian. And so God's kingdom slowly became a place I felt more comfortable living in.

Now Gary was never without blemish. Like me, he had a personal relationship with sin. He knew it, I knew it and God surely knew it. But unlike me, he had a strong desire to see more of Christ and less of sin as part of his life. He wanted to be godly—and he wanted me to be godly too.

I'll not soon forget that first time we prayed together. My first theology course took place in his den.

"Paul, Jesus is here in this room with us. See that empty chair in the corner? Picture Jesus being in that chair when we pray. He's really here in this room with us."

I gave him a funny look.

We got on our knees. We closed our eyes. He prayed. I peeked. He prayed again. I peeked again. I shrugged my shoulders. I decided that I'd give it a try; after all, he seemed to really believe that God was there. I prayed. And kept my eyes closed.

God was indeed with Gary and me in that room. And in the days to come, my new life as a Christian was not confined to Gary's den nor was Christ confined to Gary's rocking chair. We got together weekly to read the Bible. We talked about God—and to him.

One week we would study the Bible with Ross, another fairly new Christian friend. Another week we'd pray together with George, once my biggest competitor for class offices, lead roles in plays, and certain girls on campus. Other times we would enjoy the sunset on a warm, spring evening at the nearby lake as we shared problems and mutual concerns.

As numerous struggles continued in my life and new ones entered, Gary directed me to God as the one who was able and willing to meet my needs. And when he was hassled by his own struggles or unavailable for counsel, I was able to go to one of the other Christians I had gotten to know through him.

I had changed, for the good, that summer after graduation. And inside I dreaded seeing September roll around when I'd be going away to school.

College was everything I thought it would be . . . lousy, hard, and lonely. My roommate felt I deserved three hours of credit for the home correspondence course I seemed to be taking: I wrote 250 letters (I really did) to old high-school friends that first quarter. When I visited home two weeks after classes had begun, my friends greeted me with "What took you so long?"

I majored in business because I thought it would make my father happy. It did . . . until he saw my grades.

By January, I had conceded that I was the only Christian on campus. By March, that didn't concern me too much; the pressures of college had all but gotten to me. My only real contact with other Christians was when I drove 200 miles round-trip to Gary's campus and participated in the gathering he had started with another Christian guy.

But one thing happened in April that made a big difference. A very big difference.

When I Needed Him Most, Gary Was There

All year long, some guys down the hall had been asking me to smoke dope with them. No, I'd tell them. Did Jesus ever smoke dope? Then neither could I. But by April I wasn't too concerned about Jesus' welfare, only my own. I wasn't planning to say no one day after bombing out on an important geometry test.

But right before going down the hall, I called Gary. I told him what I was planning to do. He told me it was a cop-out. I told him I could care less. He said he'd be right there, then hung up on me. It was 4:00 in the afternoon. He hitched 100 miles and was on my campus by 7:00. We talked until 1:00 A.M. For several hours we sat against the side of the architecture building, watching the rain shower down before us, as I slowly, painfully, and with great relief shared my deep hurts with him. He slept that night in the dorm lounge, was back on the road by 7:00 A.M., and with the help of a trucker, was in his 9:00 class.

That was a turning point for me. God spoke clearly that evening: I love you enough that I'll send a busy student, one who needs to hit the books tonight, to let you know in no uncertain terms that I hear you and am with you.

There was much comfort in knowing I was not a six-week project to Gary, and if I didn't live up to his expectations he wouldn't drop me down a chute and say, "Who's next?"

In future days, when I would be tempted to write off this same God, to say he didn't really love me, strong memories of that evening would make it impossible. The Word had become flesh.

My relationship with the Lord improved after the April incident. As my trust in him grew, my time spent in personal prayer improved. I met other Christians (yes, there were other Christians on campus), and became involved with the InterVarsity chapter. My roommate became a Christian that spring.

Over the Long Haul

My relationship to Gary continued to grow over the next five years. We saw each other about four times a year, called when our budgets allowed it, and wrote when we found time in our busy schedules. I entertain no warmer thoughts in my mind than when I think about my relationship with him.

He's in San Jose, California, and I'm in Madison, Wisconsin: he's married and I'm single. But in a true sense, we are the best of friends.

A Challenge to the Christian

If you are a Christian, I have this to ask: Who did God use to interest you in Jesus Christ? What was it about that person that helped your interest? Was there someone who stuck it out with you during those lean times when God seemed silent and distant? Someone who didn't run away from you after he saw the "ugly things" of your life?

Was there a Gary in your life?

John 21 says that Jesus asks three times, "Do you love me, Peter?" When Peter says yes, Jesus tells him, "Feed my sheep." I'm impressed and challenged by this passage. I know how Jesus fed his sheep. He took risks. It cost him plenty.

Do you love Jesus? Then quit protecting yourself. Let God take care of all your needs. Love someone. Take a risk, even a big one. Your friendship is needed right now by someone you know. Be a Gary in his life.

—Paul Tokunaga